Miracles, Miracles, and More Miracles

Patricia Franklin Thomas

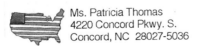
Ms. Patricia Thomas
4220 Concord Pkwy. S.
Concord, NC 28027-5036

704-784-8279

Unless otherwise indicated, all Scripture quotes noted as NIV are taken from the New International Version of the Bible, copyright © 1973,1978, 1984, International Bible Society, Colorado Springs, Colorado. Used by permission of Zondervan. All Scripture quotes noted as KJV are taken from the Authorized King James Version of the Bible.

McDougal Publishing is a ministry of The McDougal Foundation, Inc., a Maryland nonprofit corporation dedicated to the spreading of the Gospel of Jesus Christ to as many people as possible in the shortest time possible.

Published by:

McDougal Publishing
PO Box 3595
Hagerstown, MD 21742-3595
www.mcdougalpublishing.com

ISBN 1-58158-086-X

Printed in the United States of America
For Worldwide Distribution

Dedication

In memory of
Patrice Renée Harrold
My beloved daughter was a precious gift from God. Next to the Lord,
I loved her more than anything or anyone, and she brought much joy and
completeness to my life. The fragrance of her life still inspires me and all those
who loved her so dearly. She truly was my rare rose.
(January 15, 1978—October 25, 2000)

In memory of
Brother H. B. Love
This man was a great prophet of God, and a dear friend.
He would pray and fast many times for Patrice and me, holding our hands
towards Heaven and always having a word in season.
He will forever be remembered and loved.

Acknowledgments

What can I say? Reflecting on the many long hours we spent to complete this book, it could never have come together without my precious friend *Toni Bogart-Syvrud*. Her tremendous spiritual insight and revelation knowledge were great assets in helping me to write and edit this book. In addition, I would like to thank her family for opening their home to me during our efforts.

Words cannot express how much I love my beautiful niece *Katherine Marie Kress*. While I was going through a terrible physical affliction during the writing of this book, she spent six weeks with me, being my nurse, as well as helping me write, organize, type and edit my book. I drew incredible strength and encouragement from her, and even though I am Kathy's aunt, we have been more like sisters. Every morning before working on the book, Kathy would play the piano and sing, while I made intercession and danced before the Lord. After we prayed and worshiped the Lord, we would start to write. Although she is very busy, she loved me enough to come and help me with this tremendous undertaking, and I am truly grateful.

To my dear friend *Rebecca Snipes*, who was with me in the beginning, when I first attempted to write this book. She had the heart to comprehend where I was going, and would come on a weekly basis to help create the framework of the book. We spent many hours laughing and crying as we worked on the manuscript, and I am very thankful for her expertise in helping set up my web page as well.

I want to show my appreciation for *Bob Ksioszk*, better known as "Bob the builder." All his hard work was invaluable, and when the Bible defines ministry of helps, Bob would be a foremost example. His encouragement and insight helped me bring this book to fruition. I will always be grateful to him for truly seeing the big picture. I pray that he will continue to be fruitful in what the Spirit of God has already started in his life.

A very special acknowledgement and recognition to *Joyce Ksioszk*, Bob Ksioszk's sister-in-law and commissioned artist who painted the cover portrait and additional featured portraits in this book. Her gift is pure and flows graciously, and the images that remain are life altering as well as inspirational. I am amazed at the talent of this seasoned artist.

To *Jade Woodall*, I extend my heartfelt gratitude. She was Patrice's very best friend and like a second daughter to me. On several occasions, Jade would come and help me do some typing and editing on this book. She is a very talented writer and a precious friend.

To all my friends and partners in ministry: To Wade Taylor, for your kind words of encouragement and life of true witness; I will always honor and cherish the wisdom God has put in your life. To Pastors Gary and Cheryl Sheets, for being such loving pastors. To Daniel and Tammy Carpenter, my dear friends and employers, thank you for allowing me the time off work to minister and, write my story and for all the wonderful things you have done for Patrice and myself. To Larry Beaver, for your helpful advice. To Jerry Christy, for encouraging me to stay focused on completing the book, for all your help with my transportation needs to Toni's house, and of course for all your loving prayers and support. To Celeste Montgomery, my Godmother, thank you for all your encouragement. To Carolyn Atwell, my dear friend, thank you for your continual prayers, fasting and encouragement. To Bob and Hayley Roberts, who prayed and fasted for this book to be written. To Margaret Black, my piano player, friend and support.

To all those who have financially and prayerfully supported me through the years; and finally, for all the missionary teams and volunteers that so lovingly helped with preparations for the children of the foreign soil.

Contents

Foreword

The inspired writing of Patricia Thomas represents a life set apart, a witness of the wonderful transforming love of God, and the testimony of one who has persevered with unmovable faith. She has been willing to stand in the presence of the Lord at all cost.

The processing of the Lord progressively unfolds to those who are seeking to know Him face-to-face. As we turn aside to "wait" upon the Lord, our life's journey is to seek Him first, hear His voice, and learn obedience through the things we suffer. As we come to this place of emptiness, then God can begin to move and change us from glory to glory.

I know Patricia Thomas personally, and I fully endorse her ministry. God has placed His approval on her life as evidenced in the writings of her testimony, and I know her to operate in the full gifting of the Holy Spirit, with signs and wonders and a clear prophetic word. The true spirit of prophecy in the Body of Christ is to overcome with the blood of the lamb and declare the word of our testimony. Her love and trust without qualification have guided her through the years, preparing her, and her ministry, for the critical times in which we live. She has said, "Whatever You desire, Lord. Wherever You send me, I will go."

My prayer is that many will be encouraged, and come to know the Lord, as you walk through this journey with Patricia. *Miracles, Miracles and More Miracles* is the result of many prayers and tears and much hard work. It is her single desire that she will be able to say, as Paul said, "*If you have seen me, you have seen Jesus.*"

Rev. Wade Taylor
Pinecrest Ministries
Salisbury, New York

We live in a time when the existence of God has never seen any greater challenge. Yet people have never been more hungry for the supernatural. Secular humanists continue to devote great amounts of energy in an attempt to disavow and deny any possibility of divine intervention in the day-to-day affairs of our lives. The accounts in this book serve to once again prove their theories to be blind, empty and void of truth. Always remember that personal supernatural encounters proving to be authentic experiences will always supersede argument regardless of how well that argument is presented.

Patricia Thomas's life has proven to be a constant chain of SUPERNATU-RAL events, *Miracles*. Reading this book, I felt as though I was sitting with her personally as she shared each event. I found myself being drawn to a higher level of faith. *Faith cometh by hearing*. It has made me aware once again that all we need is childlike faith to see SUPERNATURAL INTERVENTIONS in the day-to-day affairs of our lives.

If you are an unbelieving person who is repulsed by the idea of the existence of a God who loves you, READ THIS BOOK! Miracles are specifically designed and performed by God to openly and visibly express His love for you. This book when read with an open mind and a hungry heart will lead you to know your miracle is at hand.

Pastor Gary Sheets
Metro Worship Center
Kannapolis, North Carolina

Part 1

My Life's Journey

SECTION I

He is a Miracle-Working God

1

What Is a Miracle?

You Are a Miracle

What is a miracle? A miracle is a supernatural intervention from God. When a natural man can do something contrary to all the laws of nature, that is a miracle. We are all natural, but when the supernatural, miracle, working power of God comes upon us, it enables us to do supernatural things through the operation of the Holy Spirit. It is not natural for a child to be born with Turner's syndrome and for a mother to lay hands on her and see the body of her child grow out to a normal size; but by faith and divine intervention, the miracle will happen. It is not natural for one to be diagnosed with a brain tumor that is hemorrhaging without the side effects of damaged brain cells, paralysis and, in most cases, death; but a miracle can change the diagnosis. Nor is it likely for someone to have no money to pay a water bill and within minutes on the same day, have supernatural provision to pay the bill as well as receiving travel expenses to preach the Gospel as a missionary to Israel. It is not natural to preach a revival, have a church respond in repentance to do its first works again, and have supernatural signs and wonders of the Holy Spirit begin to manifest; for even the pastor as well as the congregation entered again into the baptismal waters of divine glory. All these matters have one thing in common: They are all opportunities for the intervention of God to change the outcome of the situation through His miracle- working power.

A person with an experience is never at the mercy of a person with an argument. Some may question the purpose of miracles, but Acts 3:42-47 accounts for additions to the church daily as the apostles ministered in miracles. Miracles are still relevant today and are not a historical icon of the past. A miracle happens when the human soul encounters the divine touch that transforms utter frustration into a supernatural event. Miracles happen every day of our lives in the little things as well as in the monumental. When you are running in fear and something unexpected turns things around, you suddenly perceive that God is right where you are in the middle of your predicament and that He has given you a miracle! It is an encounter with the supernatural. It is where you work with God to release His power.

The real miracle is that God chooses us! We are simple-hearted, yet we are also so complex, but He chooses us to carry out His will and carry His name to the four corners of the earth. The Kingdom is within us, leading, inspiring and moving us by hope into the supernatural realm of faith. When we lay hands on the sick, they recover. When a heart is broken, it is restored by His perfect love. And when we get lost, His mighty hand rescues us.

There are millions crying out every day who need a touch from God. They shout, "Is there really a God who cares about me? Does anybody hear me? Will someone come and help?" If life was always good and we did not have a need for God to move in our lives, then we would never have the compassion to become ministers to the needy. But the cry of humanity is what God hears. As ambassadors of His Kingdom, we must arise out of our complacency and come forth. The clarion call is out to all who will respond to it. He delights in using anyone who is willing. It does not matter where you came from, what you have done in the past, or how smart and influential you are. This appointment is for anyone who will embrace it and take on the mission.

Daily miracles come as we walk with God in obedience to His Word and will. The progressive will of God is worked into our lives as blind eyes see, deaf ears begin to hear, and light comes into the darkness of our souls. Sin causes this darkness. But as we really see the sickness of our hearts, we must make a choice to step up out of our chaos into a place where God can work. His forgiveness, and grace, will set us free from the law of sin and death. In the moment we choose Him, He recreates "His order" out of "our disorder" by His perfect love. It is for whomsoever, and free to whoever will receive and believe it.

I received the call of God and believed at an early age. I have been on a lifelong journey ever since, never dreaming it would take me where I have traveled thus far. Through the mountains of struggle, but unending beauty, to the valley of troubles, from the hills of West Virginia to the lonely path to Calvary, where I found forgiveness and cleansing for my heart. I have learned in my life's experiences that the Lord Jesus has always been with me in my celebrations of life, in my failures, and in my brokenness. I have learned by going through two extremely painful divorces, and the loss of my beautiful daughter, to make the choice to walk with God. I would ascend the steps of life, suffering and struggling, and I would overcome challenges one obstacle at a time. It was there that I learned that as I took a step of faith towards God, He was taking a step towards me. In those times in my life, God was able to perform the miraculous. His love and unfailing grace for me altered my life to serve Him and become a minister of the Great Commission. I have no fears keeping me from completing my mission on planet earth. I know that I can do all things through Christ Jesus, and nothing without Him. I have the tenacity of a courageous lion when the anointing comes upon me. I realize more and more each day that the Lord has given us all as Christians a mission to win souls to Jesus Christ. However, we must not only win them to Christ, but disciple them. For me as a minister of the Gospel, there is a heavenly commission to mentor new believers by teaching them all I have learned about the ways of God. It is a privilege to teach and train them to cultivate a divine relationship; that means to honor the Lord, and put Him first and foremost in our lives.

It is as we share our testimonies of God's faithfulness in our lives that we encourage each other to keep in the faith as the Great Day approaches. He will return for a glorious Church, a Bride without spot or wrinkle. Oh, what a day that will be! My life was miracles, miracles and more miracles.

SECTION II

The Early Years

1

My Immediate Family

I have experienced many miracles in my life and I will share them with you. My desire is to expand your faith through my true accounts of God's miraculous power and faithfulness.

Patricia Lynn Franklin was the name given to me by my parents. I was one of seven children born to my mother; I fell right in the middle. There were three siblings before me: Paula, Pam and Paul Jr., and three after: Priscilla, Penny Sue and Peggy Jane. But Penny Sue and Peggy Jane both died at a very early age; thus, four girls and one boy survived. My mother named me Patricia Leigh, but when my birth certificate read Patricia Lynn, they left my name as it was, Patricia Lynn Franklin.

When they were very young, my parents, Katherine Marie Moseley and Paul Leroy Franklin, were married in Charleston, West Virginia. My mother was the granddaughter of a powerful, successful attorney in Asheville, North Carolina. She inherited her grandfather's intelligence and had a witty personality. My father was an athlete well known for playing softball and boxing. He had the looks of Paul Newman. As a young man, he was considered by many to be one of the best-looking men in town. Before my mother was thirty years old, she had a tribe, all seven of us. When I say tribe, I mean a literal tribe, because my mother's father, James Moseley, was a Powhatan Indian from Jamestown, Virginia. Although my mother was a beautiful young woman, she was faced with a lot of responsibility.

My Grandfather, John Franklin, was the owner of the F&F Hotel located in Charleston, West Virginia, which my father managed. It was a very prosperous hotel, restaurant and bar. I remember my family lacking for nothing in the early years. My mother dressed in the finest of apparel and spared nothing for her children as well. My father would buy her furs and diamonds, making sure she had the best of everything in life. Even my sister Pam wore alligator shoes at the age of five. However, by the time I was six years old, my grandfather had decided to give up the business. This left my father seeking employment that would enable him to maintain the lifestyle our family had been accustomed to.

Initially he was able to find employment as a cashier in a liquor store, but he was laid off after a few years. Attempting to establish work in other places, he eventually found himself discontented when he was unable to secure a job for any length of time. Inability to find employment with benefits caused the bottom to fall out from underneath us. In order to provide for his family, he had hopes of hitting it big, so he became a professional gambler and a pool shark. From then on, it seemed to be feast or famine for our family.

2

The Ugly Duckling

When I was two years old I developed a case of the chicken pox. One of the lesions settled in my eye, which caused me to be severely cross-eyed. There were two possibilities to correct the problem. One option was surgery and the other was to wear glasses. My mother chose for me to wear glasses, so I wore big, thick, ugly glasses in grade school. At the tender age of five, it seemed as though my only pretty feature was my long, dark hair. My sisters and brother were beautiful children, but I was considered the ugly duckling. Even though I was unattractive, quiet and shy, my sister Pam told me that she thought I was the humblest and sweetest of all the children.

One month before school started, my mother had gone to town and left us with a babysitter. The babysitter obviously had her hands full trying to watch all of us. My brother, whom, I looked up to, had a great idea, saying, "Trish, I think we ought to play barber shop." Being the obedient, kind, and humble child that I was, I agreed to be his first client and said, "Okay." I sat on the chair in front of my mother's dresser mirror, and Paul, Jr., started cutting my hair. Before I knew it, my hair was cut above my ears. The more Paul, Jr., tried to "fix" it, the shorter and more uneven it became. As pieces fell to the floor, my hair gradually inched its way above my ear, first on one side, then on the other. My bangs had been cut extremely short and were very crooked. Needless to say, when mother got home, she was not a happy camper and my brother received a well-deserved spanking. The only thing I remember was that school was to start in a few weeks, and my hair was now butchered along with my eyes being severely crossed. My glasses felt heavy on my face, and to top it all off, my two front baby teeth were missing. Can you imagine having to start to school looking like that?

It was during that summer just before I started elementary school that my music career was almost ruined. Deciding that God loved to hear me sing, I would climb up on the banister and lift my head towards the heavens, singing "Jesus Loves Me" at the top of my lungs. One day while I was serenading God, Johnny Swagger, who was one of the older boys who lived down the street, stopped and stared at me. Assuming he was enjoying the music, I continued singing, but Johnny yelled out, "Hey, Franklin!" Then he crossed his eyes and sang out in the worst voice I have ever heard. My little heart was broken and I decided to give up my musical career that day.

A few days later when I started school, the children began to make fun of me. I remember that during lunch, no one wanted to play with me, which made me feel very lonely and sad. My sister Pam, who was a fifth grader, came up to me and said that she would find someone to play with me. She talked to one of my classmates and told her that she would give her a dime and an orange if she would play with me. The girl refused her offer, and obviously, I was devastated, but what could I say? Pam tried her best to look out for her little sister; however, her little plan just did not work. As the days went by, I started to love school because I loved the learning part, but I hated and dreaded recess. It was bad enough to be considered ugly, but in addition, my last name (Franklin) became a ready source for jokes. Boys called me "Franklinstein," and laughed at me often, so I learned quickly that it was best just to laugh with them. However, that year at school, I was thrilled, finally, to find a playmate who became my best friend, Becky Smith. She did not care about my appearance, but liked me instead because I was nice. I thought she was the most beautiful girl in the world. She had long, white-blonde hair, and beautiful gray eyes.

One of the most memorable occasions in the first grade was my first Christmas play at school where Becky and I both played the part of angels. Wearing a white gown and a golden halo on my head, I felt beautiful that night. I was feeling like a real angel until a boy that I liked came up and said, "Becky looks like a real angel because she has blonde hair. You do not look like an angel because you have dark hair and everybody knows that real angels have blonde hair." I hated my dark hair and green eyes. I wanted to look like Becky; I wanted to look like a real angel. Why did I have to be an ugly duckling? Though I was very hurt by his comments, I made it through the play. I will never forget my beautiful mother who stood by my side and held my hand. She was dressed so lovely and had an aroma like the fragrance of Heaven. When she walked into a room, everyone was taken by her beauty. When the teacher walked up to my mother and me, I joyfully introduced her. She was the most beautiful of all the mothers in the room. That was definitely a night to be remembered.

Shortly after the Christmas season, my mother became ill and was unable to take care of us properly. My oldest sister, Paula, decided to move in with my grandparents, so this left Pam with the responsibility of being the mother. She did all the housework, cooked, and watched over the rest of the children. She called the shots concerning what went on at home and made the decision as to when we should go to school and when we would stay home. If Pam did go to school, she would worry about our mother and planned what she would cook for dinner. After dinner, Paul, Jr., would wash the dishes and then all the children would play together. Pam and I played our favorite game of Monopoly, which she taught me how to play when I was six years old. She decided that I could stay home to play Monopoly, clean house, and just take it easy watching television until midnight. Thus, I stayed out of school more than I attended that year, and as a result of my lifestyle, I failed the first grade.

At times, Mother would send Pam and me downtown on the city bus to pick up her medicine. It was a long trip for two little girls, but we wanted to help her get well so she could be our mother again. Mother eventually had to be hospitalized while my father continued to play pool to make a living. Life had become very difficult in our household. Before our mother became ill, she was a Presbyterian Sunday school teacher where she took us to church. When we were young, she taught us to pray and believe in God; therefore, all the children prayed for her healing so that she could come back home. As Pam and I would sometimes watch Oral Roberts on television, we would pray and believe in Mother's healing to a greater degree. Pam taught me how to read that summer. Although I do not remember the exact title of my first book, I learned to read about a peanut man who was one of the main characters. We did a lot of reading that summer, and Pam had promised God that she would read the whole Bible if He would heal our mother.

When I went back to school the next year, they placed me in the first grade again. The teacher noticed how much I had improved in my comprehensive reading skills. She was so excited about my progress that she took me to the sixth grade class to have me read before the entire class and the principal. My sister Pam was in that class and was extremely proud of my reading ability as well. After all, she was the one who really had taught me how to read. The principal was elated and my teacher requested my double promotion that day. That excited me even more, because now I was able to move up into the second grade and be classmates with my best friend Becky.

When I look back on my early childhood, I see how the hand of God was upon me protecting me. One cold winter day, when I was fairly young, my brother and I were in the living room. Trying to get warm, I stood near the fireplace.

Suddenly, my dress caught on fire and flames began to engulf me. I started screaming and Dad came quickly into the room to see what was wrong. My father, who
had been a medic in the army, quickly grabbed a rug and wrapped it around me.
Then he immediately submerged me in the bathtub in order to smother the flames.
Would you believe that not one hair on my head was singed? I do not even have a
scar from the flames. On that cold winter day, God's promise found in Psalm 91
concerning giving His angels charge over me certainly proved true, for Jesus showed
Himself strong in my behalf, even at such a young age.

Things were looking up for me as my hair grew back out, and my eyes gradually started to heal. In addition, my mother was eventually released from the
hospital and life at home started to improve. My father had a heart of gold; however, he had a problem. After spending most Saturdays drinking all night,   Dad
would come home on Sunday mornings and fight with our mother. Since Mother
did not feel comfortable going to church and teaching after her hospitalization,
we could hardly wait for the Sunday school bus to take us away to any church
where we could find peace, if only for a short while. In the safety of Mount Olivet
Baptist Church in Charleston, West Virginia, we learned more of the Lord and
we loved Him dearly.

As we grew older and more independent, all of us went to different churches.
Pam went to the Baptist church, while Paul, Jr., went to the Church of the
Nazarene. I went to the Pentecostal church with my friend Becky, who was also a
Pentecostal. When I went to the United Apostolic Pentecostal Holiness Church
for the first time, I loved the music and all the people seemed happy. However, I
did not understand the concept of "speaking in tongues." When I saw the people
speaking in tongues, I thought they all had nervous breakdowns. I was very concerned for them, so I sat in my seat and prayed for God to help them. When I
went back the second time, I really started listening to the preacher. Based on the
book of Acts, the Pastor spoke of how people were baptized and filled with the
Holy Ghost with the evidence of speaking in tongues. This teaching caught my
attention even at the early age of eleven, so I began to study and learn the Bible
for myself.

Although I was only a child, I still felt more peace being around the Pentecostal people because I could visibly see the joy on their faces. I wanted what they
had, and what the early Church had, which the book of Acts described. I pleaded
with my mother to let me be baptized in the Pentecostal church, but she refused.
She told me that when I was twelve years old I could make my own choice and be
baptized then. Eventually, I turned twelve, and my mother allowed Reverend
Anderson to baptize me in water. He recited Acts 2:38, which spoke of being
baptized. There was a promise of receiving the baptism of the Holy Ghost, and I

wanted the baptism of the Holy Ghost so much. I remember going to the altar night after night seeking for the baptism of the Holy Ghost with the evidence of speaking in tongues because it was God's promise. However, I never received the baptism of the Holy Ghost at that particular church.

One day as I was walking down the street, I noticed a paper advertising that Brother H. Richard Hall would be coming to Charleston, West Virginia. I will never forget the feeling I had when I touched that paper. It was something supernatural, a feeling that I had never experienced before. I was later to learn that it was the "anointing," the presence of the Holy Ghost. I knew I had to get to that service, so I asked Becky to find out if her mom was going to the service Brother Hall was conducting. I ask if I could go with them, and her mother said, "Of course." My other best friend, Triesa, was three years younger than I and lived on the same street as Becky and I. She was beautiful, and had the prettiest clothes I had ever seen. Her clothes fit me perfectly because I was small for my age. I asked to borrow one of her outfits for the meeting, and she graciously allowed me to pick out anything I wanted to wear. I went to the meeting feeling confidant, but most of all I had a great expectancy to receive the baptism of the Holy Ghost that day.

One of my most vivid memories of this service was that I felt the strong presence of the Holy Spirit. I was so excited, especially when Brother Hall invited anyone who wanted the Holy Ghost to run down to where he was standing. I was afraid I might miss something if I left my seat next to Becky and Triesa but I heard a voice speak, "Would you rather have them or Me? If you want Me, leave everything." I told the Lord that I wanted the Holy Ghost and ran to the front. I lifted my hands in the air and worshiped the Lord. Suddenly, I began speaking in a language that I had never heard and the peace of God came to me in such a profound way. It was at the tender age of thirteen that I had a life-changing encounter with God and received the baptism of the Holy Ghost. That was a special day that transformed my life, for I was never the same again, and I told everyone I met about this wonderful experience.

When I came home, I told my mother about receiving the Holy Ghost with the evidence of speaking in tongues. Although she did not understand, she told me something about my grandfather, Papa John, that I did not know before. She told me that my dad's father was a Pentecostal preacher at one time and that I could go to him with any questions. That amazed me to know that Papa John was a preacher, because all I ever knew was that he had owned a combined hotel, bar and restaurant. After talking with him, I found out that my grandmother had played the piano for the church before my grandfather backslid. I also found out later that the reason for his backslidden state was the death of some of his beloved children. He told God that if He took one more child, he would leave the ministry. When another child died, he ran from his call. When I told Papa John about my experience of being filled with the Holy Ghost, he was happy for me. Acts 2:39 held true for our family, *"For the promise is unto you, and to your children, and to all that are afar off, even as many as the Lord our God shall call."* Papa John was one of the first Pentecostal preachers in Kanawha Valley, Charleston, West Virginia, where I grew up. One Pentecostal preacher told me that Papa John had such a great anointing on his life. He would preach revivals in the Methodist church, and everyone present would receive the Holy Ghost with the evidence of speaking in tongues, just as the Bible speaks of in Acts 2:4: *"And they were all filled with the Holy Ghost, and began to speak with other tongues, as the Spirit gave them utterance"* .

Discovering my family history made me very inquisitive, so I asked him many questions. Inspired by my testimony, he rededicated his life back to the Lord Jesus Christ, started preaching again, and taught me so much about Jesus before he passed away. When he spent his last days in the hospital, I had the privilege of being with him on his last night on earth. As my grandfather departed into his heavenly home, I knew that I had received a great impartation.

My sister Pam had recently married but lived just down the street from us. One day I walked down to visit her and I remembered sharing with her the message of the Holy Ghost with the evidence of speaking in tongues. She got down on her knees and sincerely asked God that if this was true, she wanted to be filled with the Holy Ghost. The power of God came upon her so hard that she burst into speaking in tongues. To be truthful, although I had been the messenger, it startled me because it happened so quickly. She started going to the Pentecostal church. Her husband, Jerry Hudson, later was filled with the Holy Ghost and began to mightily preach the Word. One by one my family gave their lives totally to Jesus and experienced the filling of the Holy Ghost. This is reminiscent of Exodus 12:3, where the Bible speaks of a lamb for a household.

The first miracle I experienced was praying for my younger sister, Priscilla. The teacher had sent Priscilla home from school because she had blisters in her mouth. She was told not to come back until she went to the doctor for treatment. My parents did not have enough money to take Priscilla to the doctor, so she asked me to pray for her. I laid my hands on her and prayed, and she was completely healed immediately. The Word of God declares, in Mark 16:18, *"They shall lay hands on the sick, and they shall recover."*

Before I went to high school, the Chandler family moved to our neighborhood. Brenda Chandler was the new girl on our street, and we became close. Now I had three best friends, and she also went to the Pentecostal church with us. We were Pentecostals when being a Pentecostal was not cool. At that time, the

Pentecostal church did not allow us to wear makeup, cut our hair, and wear pants or jewelry. According to the Pentecostal doctrine, doing these things prevented people from being "Christians." When we came into the latter years of high school, we decided to try to look like the other kids. We figured we were not worthy enough, so we backslid and tried some of the other things that our peers were doing. We wore pants on occasion, and put on a little bit of makeup. However, I still always prayed to God because I loved Him dearly, but I didn't think I could live up to the expectations of my church.

In high school, as my eyes healed and my hair grew out, I was voted Miss WKAZ Cover Girl for the local radio station. My picture was on the record pamphlets promoting the top-ten song list, with posters posted wherever records sold all over town. For the first time in my life, I was developing confidence and everything was changing. The shy, quiet homely, little girl suddenly became a cover girl. I could hardly believe the changes I was experiencing.

Becky, Triesa, Brenda and I started going to dances like our other peers to become more socially accepted. I obtained a job working in a very nice clothing store, and every payday I bought a new outfit. Since I did not have many clothes as a child, this was a nice change. I started meeting many people and became involved in many beauty contests. The shy little girl that no one wanted to play with now had so many friends she did not know what to do. By this time, Paula, my oldest sister, married her childhood sweetheart, Andy Leach, and had three brilliant children. Pamela also married her childhood sweetheart, Jerry Hudson, and had one precious, beautiful daughter. While Paul, Jr. went to college and became a schoolteacher. He married a girl named Rita and had three wonderful children as well. Priscilla and I were still young and remained single.

From as early as I can remember I have always had a great love for children.In third grade I used to baby-sit for very small children. Always possessing a mother's instinct, I loved my nieces and nephews dearly. I often took my niece Kathy and my nephew Ronnie downtown on weekends to buy them candy, toys and clothes. Graduating from high school and working in nice clothing stores, I enjoyed being free spirited, fun loving and dancing with friends.

My brother first talked me into going to business school, and then later taking classes at Morris Harvey College. As I attended Morris Harvey College, a young man came up to me and told me that his fraternity had just voted me Miss Zeta Beta Tau. Can you believe the ugly duckling became a fraternity queen? The boys who made fun of me as a child now asked me for dates, but I wasn't interested. I continued to win other local beauty pageants. Beverly Moseley, my cousin, had once told me that I was the ugly duckling of the whole family, but things were changing for me, and a whole new life was waiting for me to discover.

3

Unequally Yoked

Since Brenda and I enjoyed going to clubs to dance, it seemed natural to get a job at the "happening" place where all the young people gathered called "My Place." While working one night, a band that I had never heard of before named "Ebony and the Greek" came to perform and played exceptionally well. When the band took a break, a tall, handsome young man with blonde hair came up and started talking to me. He was the saxophone player for the band, and I thought he was the best saxophone player I had ever heard. He kept asking me for my name and telephone number, so I told him my name but that I did not have a telephone. I further stated that even if I did have a phone number, I would not give it to him because I was only there to work, not to pick up guys. He asked if I would call him the next day if he gave me his telephone number. When I reluctantly agreed, he wrote his number down on a piece of paper but I ended up throwing it away, because I truly had no intention of calling him. I told him that if he was out for a good time, I was not interested in that. A girl overheard our conversation and said that if he wanted to go out and have a good time, then he should forget about me and go out with her. I had no problem agreeing with her. When his break was over, he went back on stage to continue the performance. It was obvious that he loved to perform.

The next night he was playing at the club but I did not say anything to him. He came up to me later and asked why I did not call him, claiming that he had waited all day for my call and ended up missing a good party. In response, I told him that he should have gone to the party because I made it a habit not to call guys. Again, I stated that I had no interest in going out with anybody, for the simple reason that I was only there to carry out my job. After his persistence throughout the night, I finally agreed to talk to him after my shift. I determined to tell him everything so that when he found out my beliefs, he would not pursue me any longer.

Later that evening, when he came to my apartment, I began to enlighten him on my reasons for not wanting to get involved. Explaining that I had been a Christian for most of my life, I was trying to find my way back to God because I loved the Lord Jesus Christ dearly, more than anything else. I then described the plan of salvation, baptism and being filled with the Holy Ghost, and I told him that my heart's desire was to be restored to God and get my life back. I told him that I was Pentecostal, and the Pentecostal church beliefs did not permit women to wear makeup, cut their hair, or wear pants. The dress code was the only part that I did not like about being Pentecostal. I told him that I would find my way back. He told me that all I had said made him love me all the more. So we talked for a long time.

The following evening when I saw him at the nightclub I was still a little leery of him. However, this time he sent me a dozen red roses. I had no idea what to say, so I did not say anything. Then on his next break he came up and asked me if I liked the flowers. I let him know that I liked the flowers and was thankful for his thoughtfulness. Both young and very naive at the time, we married within two weeks of meeting.

My first year of marriage was very difficult, and there were no counseling books or trusted people to speak foundational truths concerning relationships or boundaries. Idealistic at the time, I thought marriage would be a better alternative than staying at home, and I was ready to share my life with the love of my life and friend. However, it was apparent that my husband preferred to be with his friends rather than with me, and he never liked me to talk much about the Lord.

Oftentimes, when I would find myself alone and he was out with his friends, I would watch television to pass the time. The *Praise The Lord* show and *The 700 Club*, had recently come on television. God used the host of *The 700 Club*, Pat Robertson, to win many people to the Lord. I began to notice that the singers and ministers on these programs really seemed to love God and that they were Spirit-filled. Yet the women wore makeup and dressed nicely. Could it be that someone could be a Christian and still wear some makeup and dress in modest attire? I was thrilled by this, and discovered that I could now live for the Lord and be Pentecostal while doing these things. I realized that it was not about the outward appearance, but rather the condition of the heart that pleased God. I made a decision that night to rededicate my life completely to the Lordship of Jesus Christ and recaptured my first greatest gift.

After four years of marriage, I gave birth to a beautiful baby girl, Patrice Renée, which was my second greatest gift from God. My devotion to God seemed to pull my husband and me farther and farther apart. In 2 Corinthians 6:14, the Bible states that the believer is not to be unequally yoked, or joined, with an unbeliever. Because of constant strife, the Christian spouse is trying to draw the unbeliever to Christ, but the unbeliever is fighting against the call of God. Young people, choose wisely the person with whom you will spend your life. Make sure that person is in love with God first, and then with you. Remember, it is written, *"Can two walk together, except they be agreed?"* (Amos 3:3).

I would also like to strongly emphasize to my readers a familiar wise saying that I soon learned to respect in a greater measure. "Sin will take you farther than you want to go, keep you longer than you want to stay, and cost you more than you could ever afford to pay." One of my greatest regrets in life was leaving my first love, Jesus Christ, and ever committing my first sin. It didn't take me long to realize that the world had nothing to offer me but heartache, brokenness and shame.

4

The Second Greatest Gift I've Ever Had

Super Bowl Sunday is a big event for millions of sports fans across the United States, and this particular year it fell on the national holiday celebrating the late great Dr. Martin Luther King's birthday. Patrice's father had planned to host the big annual Super Bowl party. There was much anticipation for this specific game as he and his friends prepared for the night. However, God had other plans and it looked like our baby was going to come right during the middle of the historic event. Needless to say, it was not convenient to his schedule, but he reluctantly called the doctor, and the doctor told him to bring me to the hospital immediately.

The second greatest gift God ever gave me was my beautiful daughter, Patrice Renée Harrold. She was born on January 15, 1978, at 2:42 PM in New Hanover Memorial Hospital, Wilmington, North Carolina. Like all mothers, I was anxious to see my baby, to know that she was healthy, count all her little fingers and toes, and hold her close to me. After some time, I began to ask the doctors about my baby but they seemed to avoid my questions. When I asked if she was healthy, they told me that they were not sure and had ordered some tests to examine her more thoroughly. As I soon held her in my arms, I could see that her hands and feet were very swollen, and her little eyes were puffy and squinted. Her father was terribly upset and left the hospital for the evening.

The next morning they informed me that the head pediatrician of the hospital wanted to have a private meeting with her father and me. When the pediatrician came into the hospital room, he introduced himself without smiling and appeared disheartened. The news was grim. The doctor told us that Patrice had a different appearance from that of a normal child. Her hands and feet were about four times the size of a normal baby's, there was not much of a neck, and she was jaundiced. The doctors could tell by her appearance that there was a good possibility that she had been born with Turner's syndrome. They performed a chromosome study to confirm their suspicion, showing positive test results for the birth defect. As Patrice's father and I listened attentively to the doctor's diagnosis, he told us he did not know what caused this disorder.

Had the doctors suspected any of these complications early in my pregnancy, they would have recommended an amniocentesis, which is a procedure that tests for such type birth defects. Many doctors after receiving this type of diagnosis would suggest aborting the baby and terminating the pregnancy. One out of four thousand and five hundred girls are born with Turner's syndrome. Most mothers miscarry these little girls and only one out of twenty survive to full-term birth. He went on to say that one of her eyes might droop, her neck would probably be webbed, and she would be short in stature. Turner's syndrome is related to dwarfism. In addition, sixty-six percent of children diagnosed with this illness have coarctation of the aorta. Their fingers are usually short, and the average height of an adult with this disorder is four feet nine inches. I asked if there was anything that could be done to treat the illness. Unfortunately, there was no treatment available at the time she was born.

After our meeting with the doctor, my husband was devastated and immediately looked at me, saying, "What do you think of your dear Lord and Savior that you pray to every night? Your friends do not live holy like you, and they have perfect children. Is this what your God does for you? We need to give her up for adoption. Nobody will ever want to marry a girl like that with big clubbed feet." Of course, my heart was broken that he would even say a thing like that. My response was, "The Lord is my best friend. He always has been and always will be. Our little girl will be all right, but I understand how you feel. If you want to leave, you can. God gave me Patrice as a gift and she's my gift from God. I am going to be the best mother I can be." My husband was visibly upset and left the hospital, so I began to pray immediately for a miracle. Not just any miracle, but the greatest type of miracle—a miracle in which there are no questions that God was undoubtedly the only possible explanation for her healing. Hopeless situations are God's specialties.

After we had been in the hospital for a few days, Patrice's dad came after us and took us home. He was young and did not know God as I did. He had a hard time dealing with the fact that our newborn child was less than perfect. After having a few angry fits, he decided that he wanted to move back home to Charleston, West Virginia, and find employment there. We moved back home and stayed with friends until he could find employment. At least, that is what I thought, but at night, he was out painting the town red with his friends. One night he did not come home until the next morning. For some reason when I asked him where he had been, he did not appreciate being questioned. Since my friends were at work and Patrice and I were alone, in an outrage, he verbally and physically became abusive, telling me it was none of my concern. As I struggled, I looked over at my beautiful daughter who was in the crib next to our bed and prayed under my breath, "Lord, please let me live to raise my daughter." Suddenly, he came to his senses and stopped, saying, "We need to separate." He called Jerry Hudson, my brother-in-law, who was pastoring a church in Charleston, to see if Patrice and I could stay with them until we could find an apartment. Jerry quickly responded, "Bring them on." We stayed with Jerry and Pam for a few weeks until I could get an apartment in a housing project in Charleston, West Virginia.

One day while I was out, Pam received a call from my mother-in-law, threatening to take Patrice away from me. When I received the news of this from my sister, my body started trembling all over. It scared Pam so much when she saw me shake uncontrollably, she told me to go to my niece's room and lie down. While I was lying down, I started crying out to God, "Please do not let my in-laws take my baby from me!" I knew that her father's family did not know the Lord Jesus and would not train her in the ways of God. They would not love her the way I loved her, and that thought broke my heart. As I continued to cry hysterically, suddenly, the atmosphere in the room began to change. I could sense an unusual presence of great peace. Like a rush of a mighty wind, an angel swiftly appeared and began speaking to me in an audible voice, saying, "Patrice is a gift to you from God. No one can ever take her away from you, and Patrice will always be with you." Immediately, the peace of God came upon me and I stopped crying. After this glorious visitation, I never concerned myself over that matter again. God let me live, and this was just the beginning of many miracles that would take place with my second most precious gift from God, my sweet Patrice.

Section III

*The Faith of a
Single Parent*

1

Surviving the Projects

Patrice and I moved into a housing project on Hillcrest Drive in Charleston, West Virginia. I went on welfare because Patrice had numerous health problems and needed a full-time mother. My monthly welfare check of $164.00 and an allotment of $120.00 per month in food stamps proved very meager and barely sustained us. Although I received welfare, I was still faithful to pay my tithes. I remembered reading Malachi 3:10-12 as a child, which states, "*Bring ye all the tithes into the storehouse, that there may be meat in mine house, and prove me now herewith, saith the LORD of hosts, if I will not open you the windows of heaven, and pour you out a blessing, that there shall not be room enough to receive it. And I will rebuke the devourer for your sakes, and he shall not destroy the fruits of your ground; neither shall your vine cast her fruit before the time in the field, saith the LORD of hosts. And all nations shall call you blessed: for ye shall be a delightsome land, saith the LORD of hosts*". I knew that I needed the devourer to be rebuked for our sake. Luke 6:38 also states, "*Give, and it shall be given unto you; good measure, pressed down, and shaken together, and running over, shall men give into your bosom. For with the same measure that ye mete withal it shall be measured to you again*". Patrice and I had to trust God for everything.

Living in the projects was not easy. In the summer months, you would have to keep the windows open to cool off the apartment from the intense heat, and street noise and music would always fill the air. The parking lot was the hangout place in the evenings for alcoholics and drug users. They would often make sarcastic remarks to taunt me as I would come home from services, calling me things like "Holy Roller," "Here she comes!" and other names that were too bad to mention. It was a social life of fighting and strife that was habitually in the apartments and in the streets, and the police sometimes had to come to settle disputes.

I was not used to this type of violent lifestyle and would have to ask the Lord many times to protect us from harm. My little apartment was fairly nice and I tried to keep it as clean as possible. I was just thankful to have a shelter over my head, where I could raise my child and not be dependent on someone else's means.

There was an alcoholic man who lived directly underneath us, who for some reason had a grudge against us. One night while I was in a sound sleep, this man went into a rage. Taking a broomstick, he started to bang his ceiling as hard as he could, cursing and shouting at us, "You and your ugly baby, get up right now!" His words were so horrifying, I cannot even bear to repeat all of them. I was so terrified that I was trembling all over, and although I only weighed one hundred pounds at the time, my box springs rattled as I shook from fright. All I could do was pray for God to move him or me. Since I could not afford to move, God moved him within a few weeks.

The food stamps we received did not go very far. By the time I paid for formula and baby food, there were only a few stamps left and most of the time they did not even last until the end of the month. I remember one incident where someone broke into my apartment and stole our food stamps, which I had stored in an envelope for safekeeping. Unaware of this, I did my routine shopping once a month to stock up on baby food and necessary items to survive. I was shocked to find the envelope empty of the stamps and was unable to pay for the groceries. Overwhelmed, I stood at the cash register wondering how I was going to feed my baby, when a kind gentleman who observed the whole dilemma, offered to pay my bill. The Bible says, *"Blessed are the merciful: for they shall obtain mercy"* (Matthew 5:7). That man certainly was a merciful person, and I thanked him and prayed for God's blessing on him.

My niece Kathy spent some weekends with us, and the first thing she would do was look in my refrigerator and cabinets. She then would call her mother, Pam, and say, "Yes, Mom, you're right. She does not have much food." I did not ask anyone for anything nor did I want to burden others with my needs; even to this day, I just pray. Shortly after Kathy would call her mother, my brother-in-law, who was also my Pastor, Jerry Hudson, would be at my door with bags of groceries. Somehow, God made a way when there seemed to be no way. One Christmas, the Salvation Army was giving baskets to every welfare recipient. They gave me a turkey, flour, potatoes, green beans and everything that I needed to prepare for a traditional Christmas dinner. I got on my knees and worshiped God for such a blessing. Not only did Patrice and I have a wonderful Christmas meal, but I also fed many who were less fortunate than I. What a mighty God!

Her dad did not want much to do with us and very rarely came to see Patrice. Next to Jesus Christ, I loved that girl more than anything or anyone, so I tried to compensate for his absence by spending most of my time with her. I showered her with much love and attention and would teach her about God. We would spend time at the playground where Patrice would enjoy swinging, climbing and going down the slide. As I read, sang and played with her, I was constantly praying for her healing. I will never forget the challenges of being a young single parent, for life was an uphill battle every day.

God always knows what you need before you ask. One day while I was hanging up wet laundry in our apartment, Patrice was very sick with a sinus infection, which she had quite frequently. I called out to God and asked Him if He would please buy me a dryer, because I felt the damp clothes contributed to her sinus infections. I said, "Lord, I need a clothes dryer. but I don't have money to buy one and I cannot get credit approval anywhere. Even if I could, I would not be able to afford to make the payments. My family cannot afford to help at this time either, so, Lord, please provide a clothes dryer for me." I felt a release in my spirit, and I knew I had just touched the throne room of God. God was already answering my prayer.

Within minutes, a little boy who lived in the same apartment project where I lived, came and told me his mother had just purchased a new clothes dryer. She wanted to know if I needed one, because she wanted to sell me her old one. With tears streaming down my face, I replied, "How much does she want for it?" He said, "Thirty dollars." I told him to tell her I didn't have any money, but to go home and ask her if she would be willing to accept payments of ten dollars per month until I could get it paid. He came back to tell me his mother said that would be fine. They brought the dryer to my apartment, and a friend came over to install it. Miraculously, ten minutes later after I prayed, there was a dryer ready for use. The Bible declares, in Hebrews 11:6, *"But without faith it is impossible to please him: for he that cometh to God must believe that he is, and that he is a rewarder of them that diligently seek him"*.

One time there was a girl who lived in the apartment building adjacent to my place who started to befriend me. I was excited about the possibility of having a good friend who was decent and similar in temperament here in the projects. In the beginning, we seemed to hit it off, having comparable lifestyles, both single with small children close in age. She would come over frequently and borrow things, like a loaf of bread or butter, which was commonplace for neighbors to do, for many others came as well. I was so trusting and giving that, in my naivety, I was soon to find out that while I was in the kitchen, she was stealing from me. She stole my checkbook, driver's license, identification and money. As soon as I found different things missing, I would contact the police to report my stolen identification and monies. However, a month later, the police came to my door to question me, stating that a series of fraudulent checks were written close to the sum of four thousand and five hundred dollars from my account. After the initial shock, I was totally traumatized by the extensive questioning and had to convince the police that I was not the person who wrote the checks.

Fortunately, there was not enough evidence to convict me at that point. However, because her description fit mine so closely, things were looking especially incriminating. I had to really pray for wisdom, and asked God to please show me in a dream the truth of who it was, and how I could vindicate my innocence. Soon after I prayed, the Lord answered my prayers by revealing in a dream that my so-called friend was the offender. She was writing checks from my account to purchase things for herself, her family and items to sell to the neighbors. The dream was so detailed; I even saw specific items in question that were in her apartment. I was completely caught off guard to even consider her as a suspect. She didn't fit that type of illicit profile and came from a good family. I assumed that since her circumstances seemed similar to mine, things would just improve over time and she would be able to have a better life for herself and her family.

I want to stop for a moment and comment about how the Spirit of God uses dreams, as a way to reveal things you could never know otherwise. Oftentimes we find in the Scriptures how mighty men such as the more notable Joseph, Daniel and others were given dreams for strategy, insight, and confirmation of their future destiny. Job 33:15-16 states, *"In a dream, in a vision of the night, when deep sleep falleth upon men, in slumberings upon the bed; then he openeth the ears of men, and sealeth their instruction."* The Spirit speaks to us by revelation to instruct and to unveil hidden mysteries, which empowers us to find the way through the confusion of the situation. Much could be said about dreams, but it is a powerful tool given by the Spirit to equip us, and will be a sign to the believer especially in these last days. He said, in Acts 2:17, *"And it shall come to pass in the last days, saith God, I will pour out of my Spirit upon all flesh: and your sons and your daughters shall prophesy, and your young men shall see visions, and your old men shall dream dreams."*

It was because of this dream that I began to understand that it was commonplace for people in the projects to steal merchandise, reselling it for half the normal retail price, they would obtain money to support their drug habits. The dream enlightened my understanding on how to fight this battle, as the Holy Spirit gave me the strategy I so desperately needed to be vindicated. Immediately after having the dream, I contacted the police again to tell them to question this lady and I gave them in detail items that they would find in her apartment. It was hard to put in words how I came to that conclusion without appearing like an accomplice. I attempted to explain how the Lord showed me these things in a dream and that they should follow the lead. When they searched her apartment, they found the evidence that correlated with the merchants' reports, which included expensive shoes for her niece and neighbors and all kinds of miscellaneous costly items that were out of place for a person residing in a lower income housing project. As they continued the investigation, she was shrewd and evasive, and the case escalated into the courtroom and a jail sentence was impending the guilty party.

Her parents hired a private lawyer, but I had a court-appointed attorney. The interrogation discriminated against me as they started to implicate my shopping habits. The cross-examiner insinuated that I had a spending problem, often shopping with my sister. It was obvious that I had very little money, but I had to defend and account for every penny I spent and every gift I had received. It finally came to the handwriting analysis along with the assessment of the courtroom findings that brought justice, and the woman eventually had to serve time in jail after pleading guilty to get a lighter sentence.

I was upset thinking that I would have to serve time for something I did not do, and be separated from my precious daughter. The anxiety concerning who would take care of my little girl. It was more than the heart of this mother could bear, especially since I was innocent, but the hand of the Lord protected me and the heavy weight was lifted off of me. *"He shall call upon me, and I will answer him: I will be with him in trouble; I will deliver him, and honour him"* (Psalm 91:15).

Another miracle. What an awesome God!

2

Along About Midnight

It was New Year's Eve of 1980, along about the midnight hour, when I was in my apartment with my precious baby, sitting in our favorite chair together. I was meditating on the goodness of God, and as I looked at my daughter, I was reminded of the miraculous works of the Lord. After all, the odds were against her, and my heartfelt prayer was just to have her father see his daughter and the handiwork of the Lord Jesus Christ. She had stunning, light golden blonde hair and the most heavenly blue eyes you could ever imagine. I remember her wearing a turquoise silk gown that night, looking like a little angel sent from Heaven. And now more than ever, I believe she was just that.

She was truly my gift from God, but her father believed the report of the doctors. Of course, I did not blame him for believing the doctors' prognosis because he did not understand faith in God. However, I could not understand how a father could turn down the opportunity to spend time with his child, even if our relationship was over. I wanted him to perceive the God-given beauty in Patrice, and that now she was changing into a pretty little girl. God was touching her daily, and since the time of her birth, she was becoming more lovely in spite of what the doctors said. Patrice's father needed to know that Jesus was still the same yesterday, today and forever and just as He healed then, He still heals today.

I remember crying and praying that the Lord would send him to come see his daughter on New Year's Eve, so that he would be able to see, with his own eyes, the transformation. I was used to having a close relationship with God and having my prayers answered quickly. For that reason I believed that the Lord would send an angel to him the same way an angel was sent to Peter when he was in jail after the church prayed continuously. Along about the midnight hour, I was in bed lying next to Patrice, crying and praying that God would send her father to see his precious little girl. All of a sudden, there was a loud knock at my door. When I answered the door, he was standing there. I asked him what he was doing, and he replied, "Get out of my way. I came to see my baby!" I remember that he got in bed with her, and started hugging and kissing her while telling her how much he loved her. She woke up, and all of a sudden he left as quickly as he had come.

A few days later, I called his apartment, but his best friend answered the telephone. As we talked, he told me about a strange occurrence on New Year's Eve. They had all come home with their dates from the New Year's Eve party and were sitting on the couch in high spirits. Without forewarning, her father quickly jumped up off the couch and ran out the door. No one knew where he was going. I told his friend that I knew, because I had prayed for the Lord to send him to my apartment that night. I wanted her father to see how beautiful his daughter was and what the Lord had done for her. Totally amazed as I relayed the story of her father's unexpected visit that New Year's Eve, I was comforted by knowing that God still answers prayers, even at the midnight hour.

Another miracle. What an awesome God!

3

Pray, Mother, Pray

Patrice had routine medical examinations at the Crippled Children's Clinic every three months due to the coarctation of the aorta, which is the narrowing of the main artery going to the heart. Sixty-six percent of children born with Turner's syndrome have this condition, and Patrice happened to be one of those children. The cardiologist thought it was necessary for her to have surgery to repair the narrowing of the aorta when she was about three and one half years old. After consulting with the doctors, I prayed, fasted, and had other people praying as well. Her condition remained the same; therefore, they scheduled her for surgery. My heart was consumed with pain as I thought of what my daughter would be going through. I believed that God heard my prayer and would guide the surgeon's hands. My daughter would come out every whit whole.

Although I have the gift of faith, I had to walk in faithfulness through this fire, even as Job stated, *"Though he slay me, yet will I trust in him".* (Job 13:15). I remembered the story in Daniel of the three Hebrew children, Hananiah, Mishael and Azariah, better known as Shadrach, Meshach and Abednego, who were thrown into the fire. They were determined to walk in the fire whether God delivered them or not. One thing for certain, they would not bow their knee to any false gods nor would they worship the golden image. It was there in the fire that they found the fourth man standing in the midst of them, who was Christ. Despite the fact that Patrice was very young, she knew God and had a pure, childlike faith to trust Him. We both resolved in our hearts that we would not bow our knee to any trial or affliction. It was in times like this that we found our faithfulness to be tested as well as our faith.

I took Patrice to the hospital and while she was in surgical preparation, the doctors informed me that she would be in the ICU for at least three days after surgery. This concerned me because she was so young and I did not want her to be anxious, panic, or think I had abandoned her. During surgery, I stayed in the waiting room with my brother and sisters for what seemed like an eternity. When the cardiologist finally came out, he told us that the surgery went wonderfully well. Encouraging me to go home and rest since she was in the intensive care unit where absolutely no visitors were allowed, he thought I would be more able to care for her when she was released into the pediatric unit. I remember crying and hugging the doctor, thanking him for his help.

I went home praising God for her successful surgery and prayed for a quick recovery. Struggling with great fatigue, I wanted to take a hot bath, but the water heater broke and the water was ice cold, so I just fell into a deep sleep instead. The hospital called earlier than I expected, notifying me that Patrice was going to be transferred to her own room, and now I would be able to stay with her while she was recovering. I rushed back to the hospital at once and walked into Patrice's room. There she was, my beautiful little princess with tubes draining blood from her chest and IVs emerging from her arms. It is a startling sight for a mother to see her child suffering, and you never get used to it. It feels like your heart is literally going to break. Only God truly knew the depth of love I had for that precious little girl.

Worshiping the Lord with my hands lifted high toward the heavens, I would begin to sing praises softly unto the Lord and pray audibly in the Holy Spirit. Patrice awakened immediately, and would you believe my little angel received the baptism of the Holy Spirit and prayed in her heavenly language for the first time in her life? Can you imagine a little girl three and one half years old suffering great pain, but praising God? Patrice was a mighty warrior even at such a tender age and her faith in God was very well established. As the pain medication wore off, Patrice would ask, "Pray, Mother, pray for the pain to go away." I would pray and pray until there were times I would become so weary, that I would stop for a moment. In those moments of silence, she would say, "Mother, don't stop praying." So I would continue to pray and she would say, "There it goes, Mother. The pain left."

Patrice did not like having the IVs in her arms and neither did I. I encouraged her to eat some food to get the needed nutrition and strength to allow for a more immediate recovery. If she gained her strength, I was sure that I could convince the doctors and nurses to take the IVs out quickly. Playing nurse as well as mother, I began to feed her small amounts of baby food and ginger ale. Would you believe that Patrice ate and drank everything that I fed her, and did not get sick? I kept this up for a few hours to ensure that it would work, and then I conveyed her progress to the doctors and nurses, suggesting that they remove the IVs to make her a little more comfortable. The doctors agreed with me and removed them. Praise God! Another victory for Patrice! Even though she was in the healing process, she still suffered with much pain. When I think about these things, it still makes me weep.

Within a few days, they removed the chest tube, and Patrice was playing and coming back to her energetic self much sooner than the doctors expected. While she was recovering, Patrice received a little toy monkey that was dressed like a doctor. My niece and I thought it was adorable that she named the monkey after her doctor. When he visited the next day, we told Patrice to tell him her monkey's name, but he did not take that as a compliment. Oh, well, I guess I found it cute because I knew how far she had come and that she meant it as an honor. After all, wouldn't you want a monkey named after you? Released from the hospital much earlier than her scheduled discharge date, we were finally able to go home.

Another miracle. What an awesome God!

4

Cabs, Food Stamps and Groceries

While I was in the projects I did not have a car; therefore, cabs became my main resource of mobility to get where I had to go. It was hard to make ends meet on my limited income, and with transportation expenses, it became more difficult. One day I had this brilliant idea and thought I would save a few dollars by contacting Patrice's father to ask for a ride to the grocery store, or see if I could use his car instead of taking a cab. Refusing to help me, he told me that I was a religious fanatic who had nothing going for me but good looks. He continued telling me that I would have my looks until I was thirty, and then what would I do? Accusing me of raising our child to be a religious fanatic just like me, he refused to give me a ride. I burst into tears in response to his derogatory accusations. Suddenly, the spirit of prophecy came upon me: "The Lord has revealed something to me. The day will come when I have a car, and you will be without one. You will need a ride, and I will be the one who will give it to you, because I could not treat anyone like you have treated us." In a hurtful manner, he retorted, "How do you think you are going to get a car, when you are nothing but a welfare recipient?" As I hung up the telephone crying, once again my heart was crushed. So I had no alternative but to continue buying our monthly groceries and visit the Crippled Children's Clinic for Patrice's checkups in a cab.

Somehow, in spite of all these unkind words, I had faith and kept praying that God would provide a car for us. Even though I was aware of my circumstances and wasn't in any position to make car payments, I knew that God was greater than my situation. But most of all, I knew Him as my provider and miracle worker. It was shortly after I spoke with Patrice's father concerning the ordeal of the car that God's miracle for me came when a young man from our church gave me his old vehicle. I was elated; for once I obtained a car, now I would have the flexibility to function more efficiently in every area of my life. Patrice was getting better physically, and I decided to go back to school and learn computer and various office skills. I would be able to drive Patrice to a very nice day care and we could enjoy our visits with Aunt Pam and Uncle Jerry after school. Patrice loved to play with her Uncle Jerry, and oftentimes she would give her money to get a treat at Wendy's or McDonald's. She loved him so much and asked me one day if he was her grandfather, because he was always so kind to her.

Things were looking much better for us by the time Patrice turned four. Since her health was improving and she was in day care, I was now able to graduate business college and obtain gainful employment. Reflecting on God's goodness one afternoon while Patrice was napping, the Lord began to speak to my spirit, "On this day, My judgment will be poured upon Patrice's dad, because he has touched My anointed." Shortly after receiving this message from God, I received a call from her father, whom I had not heard from in a while. He asked if I would like to go to the park with him, so that we could spend some time together. It was always in my heart for our family to be reunited again, so the invitation thrilled me. I was a hopeless romantic optimist and thought maybe this was the beginning of a new start.

Our time started off as a pleasant day in the park enjoying the sunshine and riding the paddleboats. Everything was fine until he asked me to quit going to the Pentecostal church and to become a "normal Christian." In other words, his definition of being a "normal Christian" meant attending a traditional type of church instead of the Pentecostal church. His implication was that if I would deny the beliefs of the Pentecostal movement and do the more "acceptable thing," he would take Patrice and me back. That is when I responded, "You have left me before and would probably leave me again, but the Word of God says that the Lord will never leave me or forsake me. I will never deny the Holy Ghost nor turn my back on my beliefs." I suppose you could say that I gave up a man that I could see, for a man I could not see. He responded in anger and said, "I am taking you home! I can't live with you because you are nothing but a religious fanatic."

At the time, he owned a beautiful Oldsmobile Cutlass Supreme that he loved. Hastily putting us in the car to take us home, he reiterated his feelings concerning his inability to live with a Pentecostal wife. I cried because I still loved him, and hoped that he would experience salvation so that we could all be a family again. In disappointment I responded to his angry remark, "This will be the last time I cry over you, for the Lord cautioned me about your resentment this day. He said that you have touched His anointed by mocking the church that I attend and by calling me names, and His wrath is kindled against you." Not long after I said that, two young boys ran into the back of his car and totaled it that very day. We were on a four-lane highway and the impact of them hitting the car sent us to the other side of the highway. Thank God, nobody was seriously injured; however, I did have whiplash that required medical attention.

Ironically, the next day Patrice's dad called and asked me if I would give him a ride because he did not have a car now. I replied, "Of course. I will be right there." When I picked him up, I said, "Do you remember a few years ago when I prophesied to you that I would have a car and you wouldn't? I told you that you would need a ride and I would give it to you because I could not treat anyone the way you have treated us." Upon remembering our conversation, he became very angry with me and called me all kinds of names, saying, "Let me out of this car. I'm getting out!" I calmly said, "No. I will take you to your destination. I just wanted you to know how real God is." After that day, it was a long time before I heard from him again.

It is written in the Word of God, in Romans 8:28: *"And we know that all things work together for good to them that love God, to them who are the called according to his purpose."* Interestingly enough, after the accident, his insurance company wanted to make a settlement with me because of my injury. I did not go for prayer until I received the settlement because I did not want to lie to the insurance company. When I received the settlement, I paid my tithes, bought a nicer car, and had plenty of groceries to fill the refrigerator. Thus everything worked for our good just as His Word promised. The Sunday night after my settlement came, I went up for prayer, I received my healing, and things continued to get better.

Patrice was an exceptional child and there was always something very special about her. She loved to go to church with me and would intently watch her cousin Kathy play the piano and sing, listen to our dear friend Rick Parsons play the guitar, and hear her Uncle Jerry preach. She especially loved to pray for anybody who would ask her for prayer, whether in the service, or one on one. Every time Aunt Pam would get a headache, she would call Patrice to pray for her headache to go away. Patrice would always pray for her right then, and although she was a very young child, when she prayed, "sure enough," her Aunt Pam would receive her healing. On a more humorous occasion, her Aunt Pam called one day with another headache. Patrice said, "Aunt Pam, there comes a time when a person has to trust God for themselves." She then hung up the telephone and kept us all in stitches. She was quite a character even at the age of four. By this time in her life, she knew everybody and their brother's telephone number and called them frequently. As an intelligent and loving child, there was never a dull moment with her and she kept me extremely busy. She loved to go to the park with me every day, and particularly loved me reading to her.

Patrice was very active and energetic, and did not take many of my threats seriously, because I was not a disciplinarian and I spoiled her with much attention. I will never forget a particular incident that involved Aunt Pam again and proved to be even more hilarious than the previous story. One day I threatened to call Aunt Pam if she continued to misbehave. Being fully aware that Patrice knew Aunt Pam "meant business," the next thing I knew, Patrice ran into the kitchen, pulled a chair to the front door, and climbed up onto it. She then shut the door and double-locked it with bolt and chain. Amazed and bewildered, I asked, "Patrice, what are you doing? Why are you locking the door?" She said, "In case Aunt Pam comes, I won't let her in!" With clever ideas and a fun-loving disposition, her personality was ever emerging and I could not help but burst into laughter.

As a child, Patrice had a special way of bringing joy into my life. She could always make me laugh even when I was about to cry. Although we did not have many material things, we had God and each other, which was enough for me. Words cannot express the love that I had for that little girl. I have always said that the Holy Ghost was my greatest gift and Patrice was my second greatest gift.

Another miracle. What an awesome God!

SECTION IV

A Family Again

1

The Family I Always Wanted

The first time I saw Gerald, he was a minister of music for an evangelist from North Wilkesboro, North Carolina. Patrice was still a baby when he first asked my niece if she thought I would consider going to dinner with him sometime. We ate a casual dinner after church, and it seemed as though the whole church was in the restaurant eating with us (you know how it is when church lets out and the nearest restaurant fills up). Initially, we had a nice conversation and found that we had many things in common. We both loved the Lord and loved music, and most importantly, we wanted a Christian home. When we first started our relationship, we communicated daily and spent time with each other every time he was in town. Shortly after we met, Gerald proposed and I accepted, because I loved him more than I loved any other man I had ever met. However, due to some personal circumstances and decisions he made, we stopped seeing each other. It would be about five years later before we would meet again, and our courtship resumed as if nothing had ever happened. We decided to get married, moved to Beckley, West Virginia, and started our life together as a family.

In the early years of our marriage there were many years of fulfilled ministry. Always busy and happily singing together as a family, we would evangelize from time to time when we were invited. Gerald was a coal miner during the week and a music minister on the weekends. We would all practice our music daily. Gerald even taught Patrice how to play the piano at the tender age of six. He liked me being at home as a full-time wife and mother, which was my dream too, and I loved preparing meals daily and taking care of my family who brought me great joy.

When Patrice was in the third grade, she came home from school one day and said, "Mother, I want to show you something." I said, "What is it, Punky?" She said, "It is my hands. I noticed that they are different from everyone else's." I said, "Let me see those hands." She exclaimed, "See, Mother? My fingers are short and chubby, and my hands are chubby too!" I responded, "Yes, Patrice, those are beautiful hands. They are different! They are very beautiful. Your hands are special because God has anointed your hands to play musical instruments for His glory. That is why your hands are so special!" Then I kissed her little hands and she just smiled as she went on her way. She did not know that she was born with Turner's syndrome, nor was she aware that she had any differences.

Patrice continued to be a joy to our family, playing and singing with all her heart. When Patrice was in the third grade, she was chosen out of approximately two hundred third graders at Beaver Elementary School to sing lead vocals for their spring concert. Because of her exposure to weekly church ministry, Patrice was accustomed to singing in public and had no fear. Her love for singing and being the star gave her a bubbly persona that charmed everyone who came in contact with her. The bigger the crowd, the happier she was. Our pastor would say, "Now we are going to have the church's little sweetheart sing for us!" Next to the Lord, my family was precious to me, and I loved Gerald and Patrice more than anything or anyone.

Another miracle. What an awesome God!

2

North Carolina, Here We Come

Where God Guides, He Always Provides

About four years into our marriage, there was a turning point for our family when Gerald lost his job with the coal mines and was unable to find employment. At the same time, I was going to Beckley College to study a new word processing program called WordStar and take other classes such as medical transcription and medical terminology. I wanted to brush up on my office skills so that I could, hopefully, acquire a good job to increase our household income. While Gerald was out of work, he was taking any job he could find, such as painting and even cutting grass. Eventually, Gerald became very discouraged because he could not find permanent employment since the mines closed. He was going to cut grass one day and I could see by the look on his face that he was dismayed.

I will never forget one day after he left. My telephone rang and one of "Job's friends" said, "I asked God today about you." As I listened, she proceeded to critique our state of affairs, stressing that if Gerald and I had so much faith, why couldn't we find employment? She had much to say about "what she thought God was doing in our lives" and "why our faith was not working." The more she talked, the more and I could hardly wait to end that conversation and get on my knees. Immediately upon hanging up the phone in the kitchen, I went into the living room, got on my knees to pray and started to cry because I was so hurt. I said, "Jesus, people are now even doubting the gift of faith that You have given me."

Most people who know me understand that I am hurt most by someone doubting the gift that God has bestowed upon me. As I was praying, I said, "Jesus, evidently You are finished with us here in Beckley and You have other plans for us. Lord, I want Your perfect will, not Your permissive will, nor the will of Gerald's family or my family. The only way I know to ask You where You want us to go is to have my telephone ring with a call from a preacher with job opportunities for both Gerald and me." I started naming every preacher I could think of before the Lord (and I know a lot of them). There was one particular Pastor in Kannapolis, North Carolina, who came to my mind as I was praying, but still the telephone did not ring. Because I was used to hearing from God quickly after I prayed, I inquired of the Lord again and said, "Okay, God, no one has called. I know that I was not willing before, Lord, but I will even go to Africa if You call me there. I will go anywhere You tell me. Just please have my phone ring with job opportunities." Gerald was such a wonderful music minister and I knew that he would be an asset to any preacher, no matter where we went. Suddenly, the spirit of joy came upon me and I started dancing and praying in the spirit. At that moment, I knew my prayers had touched Heaven. I was so full of joy my feet would not stop dancing. I looked up and realized that my living room drapes were open. If someone would have walked by, they would have thought I was a crazy person. I danced my way right into the kitchen so no one could see me. Would you believe that the telephone started ringing? Do you want to know the rest of the story? Then keep reading. It is truly amazing!

I answered the telephone and as God is my witness, I said, "Hello?" and the voice on the other side responded back, "Praise the Lord, Sister Patricia!" I said, "Praise the Lord, who is this?" He responded, "It is Pastor Jeff Wood from Kannapolis, North Carolina!" I said, "Jeff, you will not believe this, but I just prayed that you would call!" Then he said, "Well, the reason I called is because I have job opportunities for you and Gerald." He continued telling me that he was looking for a music minister and had a man in his church by the name of Billy Davis, a homebuilder, who was in need of an additional carpenter as well. Furthermore, he told me he had a personal friend, Dr. John Diehl, who was a podiatrist in the area and wanted to hire a word processor who knew something about medical transcription and the WordStar program. He inquired, "Do you have knowledge of that?" I responded, "Yes, I have been going to college and taking classes for that exact word processing program, with courses on medical transcription and medical terminology as well." I find it amazing that God had been preparing me for that job, because He knew my future and ordered my steps. Jeff continued, "All of you need to get down here as soon as possible!" I was so excited that I could hardly wait for Gerald to get home to tell him the great news.

When Gerald returned home, I told him about my prayers and Jeff's phone call. He agreed we should move immediately, so we packed our car and headed south to North Carolina. Like Abraham who received the call, he left his homeland and followed God. There was a journey and inheritance awaiting him, but each step was to build his faith and trust in the provision of God. Like Abraham, our walk of faith takes us from one place to the next, and each step we take is one step closer to fulfilling our purpose. When you go where God wants you to go, you will find that God has already prepared a place and made provision for you. No one can take it from you, nor can you lose it. Gerald played for Pastor Jeff that very Sunday and was hired immediately by Billy Davis as well as my job opening up with Dr. Diehl and his wife, Jane. We had to leave all our furniture in West Virginia, because we could not afford a moving truck, which made it very hard for a while. We made tables out of cardboard boxes and converted swimming pool floats purchased at the dollar store into mattresses.

We had finally made it to North Carolina and the start of a new chapter was about to unfold for us. There were many good days ahead and adversities to face, but in the end, for me personally, North Carolina would be where God would reveal Himself to me in a greater measure. It would be here, that I would begin to walk out my destiny.

Another miracle. What an awesome God!

3

Only a Dollar for Lunch, But Buying a New Car

Shortly after we moved to North Carolina, our car was frequently breaking down. Not only was our car falling apart, but also Gerald had placed a board under his seat to cover the hole in the floor to keep the car seat from falling through the bottom. As I was driving home one day, I began to thank the Lord for blessing Gerald and me with employment from the very first day we arrived in the Carolinas, knowing that it was a miracle. My car was steaming as I drove down the road. I reminded the Lord of His promise in Philippians 4:19, that He would supply all my need according to His riches in glory. I continued in prayer, "You have been so kind to provide jobs for us, but now we have need of transportation to get back and forth from work." I have always been one to pay my bills, but after Gerald lost his job in the coal mines, we were unable to make payments for a few months. There were still some unpaid debts in West Virginia when we moved, so I knew our credit was not the best at that time.

Suddenly, the Lord impressed upon my spirit to pick Patrice up from day care and tell her, "Instead of going home, we are going to purchase a new car." Patrice inquired, "How, Mother?" I responded, "I do not know, but the Lord has quickened me to buy a new car." When we arrived at the Ford dealership to look at our options, a salesman approached me and asked if he could help. I replied, "Yes, sir. I am looking to buy a new car today." "What are you looking for?" he inquired. I said, " I am not exactly sure what model or what style of car yet, but I am sure of this one thing." "What would that be?" he inquired. I said, "I don't want a used car, inheriting someone else's problems. I want a brand new car."

You have to realize that I was talking big for someone that had just spent her last dollar for lunch. But nothing is too big for God and I never let a little thing like money stop me from getting what I need. I continued to go over what I wanted, describing a dependable car that provided transportation for work and church, yet affordable for our income. After looking at the different automobiles available, we both agreed that the new Mercury Topaz would be the vehicle best-suited for our lifestyle. As I picked out my car, the salesman was ecstatic to make such a quick sale until he started taking my credit application. First he inquired about my salary, and then he asked me how long I had lived in the area, which had only been a few weeks. Things were not adding up for the most favorable credit score with the combination of my salary of only $5.50 per hour and my recent move. He said, "Are you sure that is all you make?" I said, "Yes, sir." I told him we had just recently moved here, but our car was ready to fall apart literally and I needed transportation for work. He asked me how much of a down payment I could have by the next day. Remember, I had spent my last dollar on lunch, and any amount for a down payment would be too much. I was in great need of a miracle and God had never failed me. He brought me this far, and I knew with full assurance that He would bring me the rest of the way. As the salesman was sitting at his desk taking down my information, I told him that I would try to have a thousand dollars as a down payment for the car. I knew that amount would sound good enough to get him motivated to continue processing my application. He told me to come back the next day with my down payment and he would try to get the credit approved.

Now I had put my faith to the test and went home to tell Gerald, "Tomorrow about this time, we will have a brand new car sitting in our parking lot." Gerald, who was very analytical, immediately responded, "Woman, you are crazy; no one is going to let us buy a new car!" I replied, "Yes, they will, Gerald. You will see a brand new car sitting in the parking lot, a new burgundy Mercury Topaz. So, when you get home from work tomorrow, be looking for it." I continued to explain, "The salesman said all we need is a thousand dollars for the down payment. You know, I believe in miracles, Gerald." Frustrated, he responded, "Trisha, where do you think we are going to get the money from?" With my faith in action I replied, "I don't know how we will get the money, but I am going to pray. The Lord said He is going to supply my need according to His riches in glory, and I have a desperate need for a car. I am going to stand on the Word of God, believe in His promises, hold on to the horns of the altar, and watch Him move!" "Well, I'll believe it when I see it!" he replied, storming out of the room.

At that moment, I knew I was on my own and would have to trust God for His provision, even if no one else stood with me. When it comes to operating in the gift of faith, I believe that God and I are always the majority, so I kept praying for a financial miracle; it was sink or swim. I remembered how Gerald's grandmother gave his cousin a down payment on a car one time, so I thought perhaps if I called and told her the story, she would be willing to help. However, she was not able to give us the money, but she did encourage me. She said, "No, honey, I cannot afford that, but you have more faith than I do. All I can tell you is to pray. I will be coming to North Carolina to visit with you tomorrow." I said, "Well, when you get here, look for a brand new burgundy Topaz sitting in the parking lot."

Checking my mailbox to see if perhaps I had a financial miracle in it, I was disheartened to see that no mail came that day. As I kept praying, my doorbell rang about nine o'clock in the evening. When I opened the door, there was a little neighbor boy with a letter addressed to me that was accidentally placed in their mailbox, so his mother told him to bring it to me. I thanked him and opened the letter to find a wonderful surprise from my best friend, Triesa Anderson, from Charleston, West Virginia. She had sent me a very nice letter with a check for one hundred dollars enclosed. I was so happy that I ran and told Gerald, "Look, Gerald, it's a miracle! Here is a check for a hundred dollars, it's ten percent of what we need." Unimpressed, he said he was going to bed.

I stayed up and continued to pray into the late evening until I could not pray any longer, and eventually fell into a very peaceful sleep. The next day I went to work and told all my friends including the office manager, that I would soon be driving a brand new car. My office manager asked me how I thought I was going to be able to buy a new car. She wondered in amazement and told me that she had lived in Kannapolis all her life, but was still unable to get a new car. I told her I had connections with the man upstairs, but she just laughed.

As I began to work, my office manager told me I had a telephone call. It was the salesman from the dealership asking me if I had the thousand-dollar down payment today. When I told him that all I had was a check for one hundred dollars, he was not a very happy camper. He told me he didn't think Ford Motor Credit would finance the entire amount, but was willing to try for me. Irritated when I accepted his offer, he told me he would call back with an answer. Immediately, I felt compelled to pray, so I went to the office lounge and said, "Lord, I need a miracle. I have told everyone I work with, my husband and my family that You are going to get me that new car today. You are not a man, that You should lie, and Your Word says, 'ask and it shall be given unto you', and now, Lord, I need a miracle. I've asked and now I want to prove to all these people that You are Jehovah Jirah, my Provider." Suddenly, my office manager told me I had another call. I answered the phone and it was the car salesman again. He said, "Mrs. Thomas, do you still want the car?" I said, "Yes, sir!" He said, "Come on down and pick it up."

Tears of joy were streaming down my face as I asked my office manager for permission to take an early lunch break to pick up my new car. Graciously, she let me go and everyone at work was amazed when I drove back in that brand new Mercury Topaz. Once again, God had made a way where there was no way, proving to all my family and friends that He has never failed me and never will. When Gerald got home and his grandmother came to visit us, they were both very astounded to see the new car sitting in the parking lot.

Another miracle. What an awesome God!

4

Dreams Really Do Come True

A Supernatural Growth in Body and Song

Years ago, when Patrice was only four and we were still living in the housing project, I attended a special service at my brother-in-law's church. Pastor Jeff Wood, a visiting prophet and evangelist, called me out of the congregation during the service. Known for operating in prophecy and the gift of the word of knowledge, Pastor Jeff Wood began to speak prophetically. He told me that God had heard my prayers, seen my tears, and was going to answer my prayers. Pastor Wood went on to say that God was pleased with me and had told me to dream the biggest dream that I possibly could, because God was going to fulfill the dream. I knew exactly what he meant.

I had a dream that night after the service that was so vivid that it was like watching a color television presentation. In the vision at first I heard a young lady singing with the voice of an angel. As the dream unfolded, I then saw the young singer standing in a huge auditorium. I had never seen an auditorium so large like the one in my dream, so I inquired of the Lord, "Who is that young lady with the beautiful voice of an angel?" After I said that, her face started coming into focus. I began to recognize her as I came closer and closer to her. I exclaimed, "My Lord and my God! That's Patrice!" However, Patrice was not four years old in my dream, but a young teenager. The Bible states in Jeremiah 33:3, "*Call unto me, and I will answer thee, and show thee great and mighty things, which thou knowest not*". I knew the Lord was showing me what she was going to be in the future. He was going to answer my prayers and I did not have to concern myself about my daughter's complete healing. She would be anointed to sing, beautiful, and talented, as well.

That vision of Patrice influenced me so greatly that I was able to endure the challenges of our life walking in full confidence, God had a wonderful plan for her. In my dream, she was five feet three inches with cascades of long, golden hair. The auditorium was gigantic occupying all classes of people. After she sang, she received a standing ovation. Later in the dream, I was in the audience and she came to sit with me after her wonderful performance. Tears were streaming down my face, and she so innocently asked, "Why are you crying, Mother?" I responded by saying, "These are not tears of sadness; these are tears of joy. Patrice, I always knew God would bless you but I did not know that He would bless you this much." When I awoke from the dream I was so excited, that I called my sister Pam and told her about the dream. Recounting every detail of the dream, I shared that I knew of a surety that Patrice was going to receive her complete healing, and be an anointed musician as well.

Now at the time that I had this dream, there were no medical options for children born with growth deficiencies, but when you see in the prophetic, God is showing the outcome of the person's future not their present state. Therefore, I never tried to figure this out. I did not have any idea how Patrice was going to grow to a normal size, or be as beautiful as she was in the dream. But I knew what I saw in the spirit. As I prayed, the images from that dream inspired my heart for many years creating a more unwavering faith concerning Patrice's healing.

When Patrice was about nine years old, she saw advertised on television a new treatment on the market that had the potential to enhance the growth of children diagnosed with growth deficiencies, and she desired to look into the program. After contacting the clinic located in Charlottesville, Virginia, that was researching the pilot treatment, we soon became part of the study and Patrice started taking injections for a few years. Although this treatment could assist her growth pattern to be consistent with other grade school children, there would ultimately be no impact on her adult height. They clearly explained that this medicine would not alter her eventual height; in other words, as an adult, if she was only to be four feet three or four feet nine that would be her final stature. Even though Patrice and I were fully aware of the outcome, she was still interested in participating in the program.

However, I knew a miracle was waiting to happen because my gift of faith and prophetic intercession pressed me into the core of my inner man to have faith to release her miracle. There is a place where God wants us to go, where everything we do and say becomes a creative word. We must never lose the expectancy to see that creative word become a miracle. This is what most people would call tenacious faith, but I call it the "gift of faith." Oftentimes, miracles come when you least expect them. God can move all of a sudden during an uneventful evening, such as the night we came home after a revival and sat down relaxing on the couch. Patrice was standing in the hallway pleading, "Mother, my head hurts. Would you please pray for me?" As I went up to pray for her, she immediately fell out in the power of God in the hallway and began to experience the creative miracle we had all so longed for. The supernatural power of God caused her little body to grow instantly, and there was visible moving and shaking as she grew several inches. No high-tech solution, no advanced medical technology, nor anything else could compare with the miraculous, anointed, glorious demonstration of His supernatural power that healed my precious girl and caused her within seconds to grow to a normal height of five feet three and a half. She would no longer need the assistance of the Charlottesville Medical Center in Virginia, because the Great Physician had a master plan that would surpass anything man could offer—a "creative miracle!"

The Word of God declares, in Hebrews 13: 8, "Jesus Christ the same yesterday, and to-day, and forever". What He did in the Bible, He still does today. He is the God who parted the Red Sea, turned water into wine, and healed the lame, the blind, the sick and the afflicted. He was a cloud by day and a fire by night, and He is still the same miracle-working God today as He was in the Bible. The Word of God states in Jeremiah 33:27, "For I am the Lord God of all flesh; is there anything to hard for me." The God I serve is the God of impossibilities, and I can truly say that there is nothing too hard for Him. There is no problem too big that God can't solve, nor any disease too great that God can't heal. I believe in miracles, because I believe in God.

It would come to pass after this miraculous healing that keys would be given to open the doors to fulfill this dream. Nine years after the dream, while I was working for Dr. Diehl and his lovely wife, Jane, in their office, she and I started to talk. She said, "Patricia, Patrice is a very talented girl and I know talent when I see it. Patrice has the voice of an angel." She went on to explain that every year the Charlotte Hornets held auditions for the most talented people in the area to sing the national anthem before their games. She continued to encourage me to find out where the auditions were for the current year.

At that time, I was not even thinking of the dream, but I remember looking at Jane and saying, "I am not going to call them, because I'm sure every mother in this area calls them and tells them the same thing about their child." At that, Jane insisted, "Patrice is not the average child; she has a unique voice that is far superior to most children her age. I know that once they have heard her, they will choose her." Due to my reluctance, Jane called for me telling them about Patrice and scheduled an audition.

I will always remember taking Patrice to the audition and seeing hundreds of people anxiously waiting their turn. At the time Patrice auditioned, she was only twelve years old, yet she had a confidence that was unbelievable. She stepped out into the middle of the auditorium with no fear and belted out the most dynamic performance of the national anthem I had ever heard. My spirit was leaping and, all of a sudden, the Lord reminded me of the dream. That is when I knew without a doubt that my dream would soon become a reality.

I was astounded to see the expressions on the judges' faces as they listened to her sing. They could hardly believe that a twelve-year-old could have such a powerful and lovely voice. A few weeks later just after Patrice turned thirteen, she received a letter from the Charlotte Hornets inviting her to sing the national anthem in March.

On March 26, 1991, my prophetic dream came true when Patrice sang her gospel rendition of the national anthem before twenty-three thousand people at a Hornets game in the Charlotte Coliseum. As I waited in the coliseum for the event to begin, a man seated beside me started to talk. I was so excited that evening that I could not help telling him about my daughter singing the national anthem. When he asked me where we were from, I told him, "Kannapolis, North Carolina". Amazingly enough, he told me he only knew one person from Kannapolis, which happened to be Jeff Wood! Would you believe the person he knew was the same prophet who told me to go home and dream the biggest dream possible when Patrice was only four years old? Now this was the actual fulfillment of that prophetic dream God had given me so many years ago! Dreams really do come true, all you have to do is believe!

Another miracle. What an awesome God!

5

Many are the Afflictions of the Righteous

When I was almost forty years old, I changed jobs and was no longer working for Cabarrus Podiatry. My new position was working as a data processor for the Cabarrus Memorial Hospital Home Care located in Concord, North Carolina. Although I looked very healthy, I was suffering horrific headaches along with seeing flashing lights, similar to people who suffer migraine headaches. The doctor diagnosed me as having these migraine headaches and did not seem to think I should be concerned.

However, one day while I was working, I developed an excruciating headache that was different from the previous headaches I had experienced. When I could not see what I was typing and was getting weaker by the moment, I intuitively knew something was very wrong. Leaving work, I headed straight to the doctor's office and told the receptionist I had an emergency. I asked to be seen immediately, but the office was full of patients waiting their turn and the receptionist told me I would have to wait like everybody else. I tried to explain the extreme pain I was experiencing and insisted on seeing the doctor right away. Not taking me seriously, she made me wait for over an hour. When the doctor finally examined me, he misdiagnosed me as having a bad migraine headache, and said he was going to give me an injection for pain. I asked him if the injection would cause me to be drowsy, because I would have to call my husband at work to drive me home. He told me to call my husband from the receptionist's desk, but the pain was so excruciating that I could not think clearly. I asked the receptionist if she would please call my husband's place of employment and she asked, "Where does he work?" I told her, "Celanese." There were two plants in the area for this company, and when she asked which plant my husband worked at, I told her I could not remember. She was very indifferent and probably thought I was out of my mind or somewhat of a hypochondriac, so she never attempted to call him at either plant.

I could see that I would have to drive myself home, so I went back to tell the doctor I wasn't taking an injection for pain because his receptionist would not call my husband. As I drove home, I had no idea that I was a time bomb ready to explode. Actually, I was a miracle waiting to happen, but I just did not know it. When I pulled into the parking lot I could not remember how to park my car nor think clearly due to the intense pain in my head. Can you imagine after years of driving, I could not remember how to park my car? I blew the horn to get attention for help and suddenly, out of nowhere, a man came up to the car. I had never seen this man before, but I believe he was an angel God sent to help me. He asked me if I needed help and I replied, "Yes, sir. I can't remember how to park my car. Will you please park my car for me?" He proceeded to park my car and I never saw him again. In Hebrews 13:2 the Word declares, *"Be not forgetful to entertain strangers: for thereby some have entertained angels unawares"* .

Still disoriented from the pain, I found my way upstairs to my apartment somehow. My husband called me as I walked in, and I told him to come home immediately after picking Patrice up from school. Something was very wrong with me and I needed to see a doctor immediately because I couldn't even drive or think clearly. He picked Patrice up from school and took me straight to the doctor's office, as the pain seemed to grow worse every minute. Again, the doctor misdiagnosed me and told me that I was only experiencing a severe migraine headache. So, this time, he gave me an injection for pain and I went back home and fell into a deep sleep that lasted about six hours. When I woke up, I felt nauseated and sick, but it was too late to go to the doctor's office, which was now closed.

We headed to the local urgent care center, where the nurse explained that she did not think I was experiencing a migraine headache, because the pain should have subsided after the previous treatment took effect. She gave me another injection for pain and advised me to go to the emergency room to have a CAT scan. I told her I would call my doctor in the morning to make another appointment for further examination, but the next morning I woke up early only to find that the pain had intensified. I told my husband to call the doctor again, but the doctor told him to wait until noon and he would meet us at his office. Another four hours of waiting caused me to suffer pain that was even more agonizing.

I called a few of my friends who were preachers and asked them to pray. At noon, we went to see the doctor, and though I was in severe pain, he restated that

I was just having a major migraine headache and should be all right. I told him that the nurse at the urgent care center recommended a CAT scan because she suspected it to be more than a migraine headache. He said I did not need one, but because I was so insistent on it, he would schedule it with the hospital. I went to the hospital, had the CAT scan, and went to work on Monday per his advice. On Monday morning the doctor's office called to notify me that something had shown up on the CAT scan and they were making an appointment for me with a neurosurgeon immediately.

I remember as I told my coworker and friend Evelyn Story what the doctor said, she started crying, "Patricia, you have more faith than anyone I know, and if God doesn't heal you, He is not the God I serve." I looked at her and said, "Evelyn, remember that song I always sing? He is the God that cannot fail. Evelyn, He has not failed me yet, He never will, and He will give me a miracle." She continued to cry, but even in my worst pain, I was still preaching and proclaiming the Word of God. I called Gerald at work and told him that the doctor had scheduled an appointment with a neurosurgeon in Charlotte and that we needed to go immediately.

He picked me up from work and we met with the neurosurgeon, Dr. Heafner, at the Charlotte Neurological Center in Charlotte, North Carolina. He told us that things looked pretty bad, but in order to accurately discuss the diagnosis and necessary treatment, I would need to have an MRI along with my CAT scan. From the appearance of the MRI, there was a brain tumor called an angioma that was hemorrhaging. The only thing that he could do was offer surgery to stop the bleeding, but he could not promise us anything else. One very small-miscalculated move of the scalpel, and it could all be all over for me. I asked him if he could give me any hope at all. In all honesty, he looked at me and said, "No, Mrs. Thomas, I cannot. After looking over your records, it seems as though you have already had some extensive medical conditions. I am sorry and sympathize with you, but I need to go ahead and schedule you for surgery so I can get the bleeding stopped without delay."

As a precaution, I asked if I could go back home first and call one of my best friends, Brenda, an administrator for one of the most well-known neurosurgeons in Charleston, West Virginia, for a second opinion. She had always told me what a wonderful doctor he was and how he would pray for every patient before he did surgery. I felt if I had to have surgery, then I needed to be around my family. Since most of them were from Charleston, I thought I would ask him to perform the surgery. When I spoke with Dr. Amores, he asked me to tell him exactly what Dr. Heafner had disclosed concerning my prognosis. When I relayed the details of what the neurosurgeon had told me, Dr. Amores responded by telling me that

I needed to be admitted to the hospital immediately and that this condition was extremely critical. I asked him if he would do the surgery, because I knew he was one of the best in his field. He stated that Charleston did not have the state-of-the-art equipment that was available in Charlotte, but more importantly, I probably would not even survive the trip to West Virginia. He mentioned that I could be thankful that Charlotte's facility would be better suited to treat me, but that approximately one out of three hundred and fifty thousand people with such a diagnosis did not even survive such a thing. Most people in this condition die immediately; nevertheless, if a person was fortunate enough to survive the surgery, they were usually blind and paralyzed on one side. As he inquired more about the doctor's prognosis, I told him that Dr. Heafner said he could make no promises and implied that I might be a vegetable if I lived. Dr. Amores asked me if there was anything he could do for me. I told him, "Yes, please pray for me." I told him that Brenda shared with me how he always prayed for his patients, so he said he would pray for me.

Once more, I had my faith tested. Hebrews 11:1 declares, *"Now faith is the substance of things hoped for, the evidence of things not seen"*. I relayed my conversation with Dr. Amores to Gerald, which completely traumatized him, and then contacted my Pastor, Jeff Wood, to tell him of the situation and ask him to pray. He said he believed that I would live and not die because too many prophecies had gone forth about my life that still needed to happen. I called Brother Hall and my brother-in-law, Pastor Jerry Hudson for prayer. Brother Richard Owings prophesied that I would live. Rev. Thelma Wilkins, my dear friend, prayed for me as well. I asked her to not give up on me and to keep praying until I received my miracle, to which she promised she would. That was one day the phone company was making direct connections with Heaven through the many preachers and friends who prayed at my request.

My husband was also calling and asking everyone to pray for me. Even my co-workers were praying. I remember asking the Lord, "Please make this cup pass from me," but then I quickly repented. I said, "No, Lord, if this trial I am going through will cause one soul to be saved, healed or delivered, I am willing to go through it. Just bring me out every whit whole." Then I promised God that I would not just sing and testify anymore, but I would preach the Gospel uncompromisingly.

I then called Dr. Heafner's office to schedule the surgery date, and was informed that I needed to come in a day earlier for the preparation. The day before I went to the hospital, I was lying on the couch meditating on the goodness of God while my husband was pacing the floor concerned about finances. Not knowing how was he going to get back and forth from work every day, visit the hospital, and take care of Patrice, at the same time, he became apprehensive. In addition, he knew that the recovery would take weeks or even months, if I even survived. I asked him to quit pacing the floor because I knew God would make a way where there seemed to be no way. I reminded him that we always paid our tithes and that now God would take care of us. I began to pray and asked God to please give us a financial miracle that day, so that Gerald would have plenty of money for gas to go back and forth to the hospital. I also asked the Lord if He would please help me buy a new gown, robe, and house shoes to take to the hospital. As I felt a release in my spirit, I knew I had touched the throne room of God and told Gerald that God would soon move.

A few minutes later, my telephone rang and it was my friend Evelyn asking if she and another friend could come and visit. They came later that afternoon and brought me four hundred and twenty-four dollars that was taken up in a collection for me at work. The two of them were crying as they were leaving thinking that this might be the last time they would ever see me. I assured them, "I am not going to die but live. God is going to give me a miracle, so please do not feel sorry for me. God has never failed me." The other friend told me that when she was my daughter's age, her mother also had a brain tumor and after surgery, she was left blind and paralyzed on one side. While they were crying hysterically over Patrice and me, I reiterated, "Please do not cry. That is not going to happen to me because God is going to give me a miracle." They hugged me and left.

After they left, we both went to pick up Patrice after school and then went to Belk's to buy a new robe, pajamas and house shoes, making sure they all matched. When I got home from shopping, another friend called and asked if she could come over. She had a beautiful box wrapped for me; when I opened it, I was amazed, because the gown she bought matched the robe and pajamas I had just bought. Isn't that just like God? They were the same brand name, color and style! He really does know everything, for not only did He supply all of my needs, He even made sure it was all coordinated perfectly, because everything God does is perfect and in order. That is how much my Lord loves us and cares for every specific detail that is important to you.

One of the last things I did before the evening ended was to ask Gerald to turn the music equipment on so that we could make a tape for all the people who had prayed for me. We had a keyboard and an entire sound system in our living room where we practiced daily. At that time, we did not have anything to give anyone, except our talents, so we did just that. Anyone who knows me, knows that I am a big giver and I have been known to give away just about all that I have to bless someone else. Gerald began to play and then God put in my heart what songs to sing. We named the tape "Songs of Faith", which included the following songs:

"There Is a Miracle in the Making," "Fear Not, My Child" and "The King of Who I Am."

The telephone began to ring right after we finished recording and Gerald picked up the phone. It was Brother H. B. Love, a prophet and minister from Concord, North Carolina on the other end with an extremely timely message for me. I do not know why I did not think to call Brother Love for prayer, but I was to soon understand the importance of this call, for it was better that he did not know my situation so that he could speak directly to the spirit of infirmity by faith. Brother Love began to relay to my husband that the Lord showed him that Satan had an all-out war against our family and was trying to kill me. He wanted to talk to me directly, saying, "You are not a prophet but your wife is, and she will understand. Let me talk to her!" When I picked up the line, Brother Love repeated his conversation with Gerald concerning the devil trying to kill me and then asked me what was going on. I conveyed the doctor's prognosis concerning the brain tumor hemorrhaging and the chances of my survival. If I lived through it, they thought I would be blind and paralyzed on one side and most likely would have damaged brain cells. I also told Brother Love I was not afraid, for I knew God would heal me. I would not be paralyzed or blind but would live, and I did not want to have damaged brain cells either. I knew that God would heal me, because the Word of God declares, in Psalm 34:19 *Many are the afflictions of the righteous; but the Lord delivereth him out of them all*. Brother Love told me that this affliction was not unto death, but that the Lord was going to use this trial to begin a new ministry for me. The Lord would give me a miracle and I would not have any damaged brain cells. He proceeded to tell me about the doctors and things that would be going on throughout the surgery. I knew this was a true word of God, because Brother Love had no idea that I was afflicted until the Lord showed him.

Later that night my niece Kathy came in from West Virginia to be with me during the adversity, and in the morning Gerald, Patrice, Kathy and I went to Charlotte for me to be admitted to Charlotte Memorial Hospital. I remember the secretary in the admission area asking me if I wanted to sign a living will, which would authorize the doctor to take me off life support if I was comatose. At that point, I said, "Absolutely not! I am expecting a miracle. I will live and not die!" After the hospital admitted me, they took me to preop to perform tests and started by making an incision in my side. In order to take pictures that would enable the doctor to locate the exact place where the angioma was and where it was hemorrhaging, they had to maneuver a tube from my side that would extend from my aorta to my brainstem. The doctor asked me if I wanted some Valium given intravenously, because this course of action could be very painful, but my response was, "No, sir. The devil has an all-out war against me and he is trying to kill me. I need to have a sober mind, be alert, and know how to pray. Also, Doctor, if you don't mind, tell me what you see so I will know how to pray." I said this because 1 Peter 4:7 says *"Be ye therefore sober, and watch unto prayer."*

A doctor, nurse and three other male assistants were helping with this procedure. I remember the doctor saying, "I see damaged brain cells on the left side." He also asked his assistants to come and look and they agreed on the diagnosis of damaged brain cells. That is when I asked the doctor again, "Do you mind if I pray?" He said, "No." I started praying in the Holy Ghost; in other words, I was praying in unknown tongues as the Bible speaks of in Acts 2:4. I asked God to destroy the damaged brain cells and create new ones. The procedure was soon over and they wheeled me out to a waiting area where Gerald, Patrice and Kathy were. I had to be immobile for a few hours. The nurse who was attending to me looked at me and I said, "Nurse, they tell me that I may not live after tomorrow and if I do live, there is a good possibility that I will be blind and paralyzed on the left side." Then I prophesied to her, "But I tell you that I will not die but will declare the works of the Lord and I will not be blind or paralyzed. I will be in my own private room the next day eating breakfast, lunch and supper." She just looked at me in amazement. My husband looked at her and said, "Do not pay any attention to her; it's the drugs." In other words, he was embarrassed because he did not believe the prophecy. Instead, he believed the doctor's report. I said, "No, Gerald, it's not the drugs. What you do not understand is, I did not let them give me any drugs. This is the Holy Ghost speaking prophetically." Things got very quiet. The nurse looked at my niece and said, "Do you believe her?" My niece responded, "She is my aunt and I believe anything she says. If she said it, I believe it." The nurse asked my niece if she would come and tell her tomorrow if my prophecy did indeed come to pass.

They took me to my private room where the neurosurgeon, Dr. Michael Heafner and his nurse were waiting for me. After studying the angiogram thoroughly, Dr. Heafner told me in the presence of my family that as a result of the location of the angioma, there would be a very good chance that I would wake up blind on the left side after the surgery. He could not promise anything. I looked at my family and they looked like they were heartbroken. They were about to cry when all of a sudden the gift of faith rose up in me, and the gift of prophecy started flowing again; I was on a roll. I started prophesying to Dr. Heafner and said, "No, Doctor, I will not be blind or paralyzed and I will have 20/20 vision. I will be able to walk and talk, and furthermore, I will be in my own private room the next day eating breakfast, lunch and supper." The doctor said, "No, you won't." In addition, I said, "Yes, sir, I will, because of the Lord's stripes; by His stripes I am healed." He then shook his head and said, "No one has ever come out of the intensive care unit in less than three days with the type of surgery you are having, and you will not either." I again repeated to him, "Yes, sir, I will." Being the professional he was, he was just trying to make sure that when I awoke, I would understand all the possibilities of being blind and paralyzed from the surgery. He explained that other doctors were on call for weekend duty and assured me that they never let anyone out of ICU in less than three days postsurgery. He then said again, "Mrs. Thomas, I am very concerned about your eyesight." That is when the gift of faith rose up in me again and in an even more powerful way than before. I pointed my finger at him and said, "Doctor, concern yourself no more, because the Lord just showed me I am going to come out of this every whit whole. I am going to be praying for you and the Lord is going to guide your hands." He then shook his head and walked out of the room.

You might ask if I ever doubted the word that God put in my spirit. My answer to you is no, not ever. If God said it, then I believe it, like Abraham, as the Bible says, in Romans 4:20-21, *"He staggered not at the promise of God through unbelief; but was strong in faith, giving glory to God; and being fully persuaded, that what he had promised, he was able also to perform."* I was truly fully persuaded that what God had promised, He would be able to perform, and I would be strong in my faith. Once God shows me something in my spirit, I never doubt it. I knew I wasn't going to be blind, nor was I going to have any pain, and I didn't. God never has nor will He ever fail me.

I remember different people coming into my room telling me that I would be bald headed and in a diaper the day after my surgery. I also had people ask me if the doctors thought I might be blind because of where the tumor was located. Even though I realized they may have meant well and did not want me to wake up shocked of the outcome, their comments did not affect the faith that I had in my God. I was hanging on to the horns of the altar and my faith in Jesus had to go beyond the faith of the doctors, friends, family, and ministers. I knew God had not taken me this far to let me down now. His word declares, in Exodus, 15:26 *"I am the Lord that healeth thee"*.

I had such a desire to live and wanted to declare the works of the Lord. I knew no one would love and take care of Patrice the way that I could. I was determined to live and fulfill my destiny as a minister of the Gospel of Jesus Christ. I wanted to raise my beautiful, talented, and anointed daughter with all the love a child deserves. Next to Jesus, I loved Patrice more than anything and wanted her to know always that I would be there for her. God loved me enough to let me do just that and take care of my lovely daughter, what an awesome God.

The next morning they came to take me to surgery. I looked at Patrice and said, "Do not worry about Mother, Punky, because I will not feel any pain, and

God is going to bring me out every whit whole." Then I was off to surgery. I told Gerald the night before that while I was in surgery; I wanted him to play the tape we made, "Songs of Faith." I felt that this would bless my pastor and my family while they were waiting for me. While in surgery, it was just as Brother Love had prophesied. The surgery was very tedious and the doctor had to call for the assistance of another surgeon. The surgery lasted approximately five and one halfhours. "One minute miss of the scalpel and it could be all over for me," the doctor warned.

Finally, after the surgery was over, they took me to the Neuro ICU ward to monitor my stats and progress. I awoke with tubes in my neck and in the back of my head. A large strip of hair was shaved in the center of my head, and the back of my head was stapled together. Other tubes were going in and out of me in every direction. I could not feel any pain; all I could feel was the glory of God. I looked at the nurse and she said, "I can't believe this. Your vital signs are better than mine." I looked at her and said, "I'm hungry. Would you please get me something to eat?" I remembered the story of Jairus's daughter in the Bible, where Jesus raised the little girl from the dead. He told her family to get her something to eat. He knew her body needed nourishment. The nurse said, "I am not allowed to give you anything. If you would get sick, it could cause a lot of complications." She explained the rules. I told her I was very hungry and promised her I would not get sick if she would give me something to eat, but if she did not, I would get sick because my stomach was empty and burning. I told her my testimony and she was quite amazed. I continued to share about how if God could bring me this far, He certainly was not going to let me get sick from having milk and crackers. Would you believe I made a believer out of her? She was so blessed that she agreed to bring me milk and crackers. I talked to her about the Lord all night. The next morning the doctor who was on call for Dr. Heafner came into the room. He introduced himself and began to examine me. I said, " Look, Doctor, they told me I might not live, and if I did, it would be a good possibility that I would be blind and paralyzed on the left side." Enthusiastically, I told the doctor, "I am not blind, nor am I paralyzed." He looked at me with a smile and said, "Why don't you let me be the judge of that?" He then handed me a newspaper and told me to read it. I read it perfectly with no problems. I started to move my legs up and down. I looked at the doctor and said, "I told you that I am not blind or paralyzed." He began to ask me questions. "Okay, who is the president of the United States?" He wanted to make sure that all of my ducks were in a row and that there was no brain damage. I answered, "President Bush," and then I said,

"Doctor, I am going to go a step further and tell you who the next president is going to be." He then chuckled, "Okay, who is it going to be?" I replied, "Bill Clinton."

That is when he looked at me and looked at the attending nurse and told her, "Get her out of here and have her taken to her own private room. Any woman doing this well does not belong in the Neuro ICU ward." The nurse sent for an assistant to take me to my own room. As they were taking me to my room, my family was in the hallway. I remember looking at my niece and saying, "Kathy, did God deliver the three Hebrew children?" She said, "Yes." I proclaimed, "He delivered me!" I started waving my arms and kicking my legs up and down and stated, "I told you I would be in my own private room and I would not be blind or paralyzed!" I will always remember the beautiful smile that broke forth on her face.

Once I was in my private room, I was so excited about my miracle and wanted to tell everyone about it. A nurse came in to check my vital signs, so I began to tell her about my miracle. She enjoyed hearing the story, but she was very busy. She was getting ready to leave the room to check on other patients on the floor when suddenly the Lord started showing me something. I entreated her, "Nurse, please do not leave yet. The Lord is showing me that someone is going to buy me a new couch. The Lord also wants me to write a book and tell of the many miracles that He has done in my life, and I suppose He wants this story in it as well. Will you please verify that I prophesied this to you when it comes time for me to write the book? That God is going to buy me a new couch." She answered, "I certainly will." I noticed that she was looking at me strangely, as if to say, "Lady, what is the big deal about a new couch?" I responded to her silent words, "What you don't realize is that you are looking at a lady with a couch that is about twenty-two years old and has a spring dangling out of it. If I get a new couch, it will be a miracle!" She laughed at me about this, but I was serious. I knew it would be a miracle. Would you believe after the nurse left my room my dear friend Rev. Thelma Wilkins called my room and told me that she had bought a new couch for me because the Lord told her to? Not only did I receive a miracle in my body, but I also received a new and beautiful couch.

My recovery was amazing. I was eating and thinking clearly as I had prophesied to the doctors and nurses before surgery, other patients in the hospital heard about my miraculous recovery and started calling me for prayer. Although there were tubes going in and out of me, and my head was stapled, I may have appeared pitiful, but I was far from it. Full of faith and the power of the Holy

Ghost, I felt no pain. I asked the nurse not to give me any pain medication. In addition, I asked her to document this in my medical records, because the Lord had touched me and made me every whit whole.

After a few days in the hospital, they sent me home. The next week, I went to the doctor's office to have the staples removed. Inquiring about the damaged brain cells the other doctor and assistants saw while performing the angiogram, Dr. Heafner reassured me that there were no damaged brain cells to be found. Within six weeks I was back at work as if nothing had ever happened. The entire time I was in this trial, I worshiped God and gave Him glory for He alone is worthy.

Another miracle. What an awesome God!

6

Study to Show Yourself Approved Unto God

After my miraculous recovery and all the amazing things that had happened, I thought Gerald, Patrice and I were destined for a worldwide ministry. I believed we would sing, testify and minister all over the world together. Full of zeal and the gifts of the Spirit that were working through me, I was full of faith, but I realized that I did not really know the Word of God well enough to preach as I should.

My friend Catherine McLain recognized the call of God on me and thought it would be beneficial for me to attend Faith Bible College in Kannapolis, North Carolina, to increase my knowledge of the Word of God. She suggested that I should enroll and she would attend too. When she made the suggestion, I thought, the very audacity that Catherine had; after all, God had restored new brain cells for me, and God had done so many other miracles for my family. I thought that I was ready to swim in the river of God, but in reality, I was just standing on the banks looking at the water. I needed a balance. I had the gifts and Gerald had the ability to preach. So, I thought giving my testimony and saying a few words was good enough. What I did not realize at the time was that Gerald would not be with me someday and I would have to preach the Word by myself. After praying about Catherine's suggestion, I felt compelled to go to Faith Bible College and study the Word. As the Bible says, in 2 Timothy 2:15, *"Study to show thyself approved unto God, a workman that needeth not to be ashamed, rightly dividing the word of truth"*.

I will never forget the Lord speaking to me concerning the night of graduation. It would not be like any other graduation; nor would it be just a ceremony, but a miracle service. I told Catherine about this, and she replied, "No. They always have a specific ceremony where each student gets to preach for fifteen minutes. Then a certificate of completion is given to each student and a reception is held afterwards." Again, I prophesied to Catherine, "God said that it would be a miracle service."

I remember all the students giving their sermons and then it was my turn. As I was preaching, a prophet who was the special guest speaker for the graduating class stood up and interrupted me by saying, "Sister Patricia, I feel led to relinquish my time of speaking so you can hold a miracle service tonight." In respect for my teachers, I turned around to ask them if I could obey the prophet, to which they agreed.

Suddenly, people started coming up front for prayer and deliverance. One man who had psoriasis for many years experienced total healing that night. Another young man had a stuttering spirit and was totally set free. There was even a Presbyterian man who did not believe in the manifestations of the Spirit but stood amazed as he watched his son receive healing. Needless to say, he, along with most of them, were slain under the power of God that miraculous night.

Another miracle. What an awesome God!

7

Working With a Great Prophet

Two weeks before meeting Brother Shinn, the Lord gave me a dream. In this dream, I was in a foreign country. Gerald and I walked into a room, and as soon as we walked in, a door slammed shut behind us. There was a lady sitting in the middle of the room who had the power of Satan so strong in her that she had caused the door to slam shut and lock. Terrified, Gerald and I were both reaching for the doorknob in an effort to get out of the room, but we could not get the door open. At that time with great boldness, I said, "Gerald, let go of the door." When he let go of the doorknob, I put my hands on it and said, "In the name of Jesus, I command you to open." The door opened with no problem. I remembered pulling that woman out of the room commanding every demon to come out of her and she received her full deliverance.

Two weeks later, Gerald came home from work and told me that he had met a man at work who had come to his grandfather's church when Gerald was a little boy. He told Gerald his name was James Shinn. Gerald wanted me to meet him, so he invited them to come and visit. I will never forget when Brother Shinn and Jackie came to our home for the first time. Gerald began playing the keyboard and Brother Shinn began to prophesy. He told us that he had been ministering in deliverance and casting out demons for the past several years, which caught my interest. I then remembered the dream that I had two weeks before meeting Brother Shinn. I knew God had placed Prophet Shinn in our lives to help prepare me for a ministry of deliverance that I had never experienced before.

As Brother Shinn was talking and sharing with us different experiences he had encountered in the ministry, the Spirit of the Lord was leaping inside of me. I told him, "If you will hold a service, I will rent a building and will have that building filled up with people". He wanted Gerald, Patrice, Jackie and me to lead worship and he would preach. We felt that would be a great opportunity for all of us.

With the building filled to capacity at the first service, God was using Brother Shinn mightily to prophesy to the people. It was a glorious service with beautiful music, and a powerful demonstration of the Holy Ghost was evident. He asked me to minister with him, and as we laid hands on the people, they were falling under the power of God. It was glorious. Everything seemed fine during the first few services, but then things began to change drastically. Demons began to manifest through people, and this was something that I had never seen or experienced before. One lady fell on the floor and her body started slithering like a snake. She began to be uncontrollable and, truthfully, I was literally terrified. Gerald kept playing the keyboard and Jackie and Brother Shinn started ministering to her. He asked for all of us to come and help. I wanted to run; however, there was no place to run. That was my first real training session in the deliverance ministry. After that experience, I began to increase my understanding of the deliverance ministry, studying books by Norval Hayes and Lester Sumrall.

Working with Prophet Shinn and Jackie for one year, we ministered deliverance to many people and saw them set free by the power of Almighty God. I will forever be grateful to Prophet Shinn and Jackie for the impartation and teachings of the ministry of deliverance. Little did I know just how much my time with them would truly be a treasure of God to prepare me for ministry in the future and how my destiny would be affected.

Another miracle. What an awesome God!

8

The Spirit of the Lord Is Upon Me to Preach

In this journey of identifying the call of God for my life, so many great women in the Bible inspired me with admirable character . Deborah, for example, stirred up the people from their apathy, and her legacy of wisdom and discernment made her known near and abroad. She was the exemplary *"mother in Israel,"* and *"the children of Israel came up to her for judgment"* as she sat in her tent under a palm tree *"between Ramah and Bethel"* (Judges 5:7 and 4:5). Abigail, whose story is found in 1 Samuel 25, because of her great prudence and delicate handling of a critical period of her husband's life, obtained the testimony of not only being beautiful, but most importantly, *"a woman of good understanding."* Esther, one of my favorite examples of a woman of great faith and courage, saved a whole nation because of her true obedience and humility before God. My heart's desire was to be known in God's Kingdom as an exemplary mother in Israel, a woman of good understanding and whose courage could save many nations because of obedience and humility.

To preach the Word of God, to me, is one of the greatest honors and callings, and now I was elated to receive an invitation to preach at the Salisbury Women's Aglow in Salisbury, North Carolina. We were still working with Brother Shinn and Jackie, but this was an opportunity for me to preach. When I shared the news with Brother Shinn and Jackie, he told me that he would go and be a "catcher" for the people as I ministered to them when they would fall under the power of God. We had always worked under Brother Shinn, and this was quite a big difference for him to be serving in this capacity as I ministered.

We were going to minister as planned with Gerald leading worship and me singing with him. Then, after worship, I would give my testimony and have ministry time at the end of the service. However, God had other plans. Before I gave my testimony, God began to use me in the gift of word of knowledge and healing with prophecies. I could sense the boldness of the Holy Spirit come upon me, as so many of our heroes of faith experienced. I began to understand the wisdom of God when He moved on the prophetess like Deborah. As with her, the spirit of revelation and prophetic word would be similar to a plumb line, bringing godly guidance, deliverance and healing to the people. So often, we think of God as far away, or so holy and sovereign that He is not concerned with all our small matters, such as our losses, our heartaches and our tragedies. There He was in the midst of us all. To my surprise, almost all of the ladies were lying on the floor under the power of God.

I have to laugh when I think about what my husband said to me. He looked at me and said, "Trisha, hurry up and preach and give your testimony." I remember looking at him and I could not help but laugh as I responded, "Gerald, who am I supposed to give the testimony to? They are all out in the Spirit." I was amazed at the power of God. I just kept laughing with the joy of the Lord.

Who would ever have believed that this little, timid woman, who was at one time on welfare and living in a housing project, would one day be ministering under such a supernatural anointing.

Another miracle. What an awesome God!

9

A Vision of Me Being on Television

One day, Gerald and I went out to lunch with some friends of ours. While everyone talked, the Lord quickened in my spirit that I was going to be on television giving my testimony. I shared what God had spoken to my spirit about getting a call to share my testimony on a Christian television program. They all laughed and said, "Sure. Right." I said, "Go ahead and laugh if you want to, but I know the voice of God." I received a phone call from Pastor Jeff Wood that evening when we got home asking me if I would go with him and his wife to Greenville, South Carolina, to share my testimony of the many miracles God had performed in my life. On the following Monday, I was sitting in a television studio just like the vision God had given to me.

The following weeks after I shared my testimony on television, people were calling me for prayer and many were writing to me. I received one very special letter from a lady by the name of Margaret Black. She was going through a difficult time in her life and shared with me about how brokenhearted she was over the situation. My heart was overwhelmed with compassion for her. Therefore, instead of writing her back, I chose to call her on the telephone immediately. I ministered to her and she was very grateful. The Word of God says, in Romans 8:28, *"And we know that all things work together for good to them that love God, to them who are the called according to his purpose"*.

She wanted to know when I would be ministering again. I told her my family ministered every weekend with Prophet James Shinn and his wife, Jackie. Margaret and her husband came to the next meeting. She also told me that she had played the piano since she was nine years old in Pentecostal churches and would love to play for me if I ever needed a pianist. I told her I really appreciated her offer, and would keep that in mind, but I was married to a music minister who always played for other evangelists and for me.

At that time, I did not realize that one day Gerald would leave me and I would have need of a piano player, but God did. I believed it was not just a coincidence but also a divine appointment for Margaret Black to turn on Channel 16 the night I was giving my testimony. God knew that someday not too long after that, I would need a piano player. He loved me enough to direct Margaret to watch the program.

Another miracle. What an awesome God!

Open Vision at The Benny Hinn Crusade

I attended a Benny Hinn Crusade in Atlanta, Georgia. I literally went into an open vision *"whether in the body or out of the body, I cannot tell,"* just like the apostle Paul said, in 2 Corinthians 12:3. In the vision, I experienced being caught up into the realm of the Spirit of God, with Jesus. I saw the Lord sitting behind a desk, and I was sitting in a chair in front of Him. It was like the Lord was my personnel manager and I was in middle of being interviewed for a position. The Lord speaks to each one of us individually in a language we understand. Since I had worked many places from the time I was a young child, this was my language. Because of my experience interviewing with many personnel mangers, I knew what they liked to hear. They want to hear what you can do for them, not what they can do for you. That is the way to find favor and obtain employment. So many Christians are interested in what God can do for them but should be more concerned with what they should do for God.

That is when I began to inquire of the Lord. I shared with Him the reasons why I had such a great desire to work in His Kingdom. Believing that hell is for the devil and his demons and Heaven is for God and His children, I wanted to win millions of souls to the Kingdom of God, which is my heart's greatest desire. I still to this day want to minister healing to the sick, deliverance to the depressed and oppressed, operating in miracles, signs and wonders to His children. These desires have all but possessed me and I pray for these things daily. I love God dearly, and next to Him, I love all of His children. I know I can make a difference in the lives of people because of the great love I have for Jesus and His children. I asked Him to hire me in the ministry full-time and to please pay me the amount of money I was making or more working as a full-time medical transcriber in a medical office. This would help me meet our budget and keep Patrice in music lessons and Christian schooling.

There were many other reasons for my desire to work in full time ministry. He had performed so many miracles for my family and me. I told Him I did not need a vacation or a break, but for Him to just please hire me. After working all day, coming home, cooking, taking Patrice back and forth to music practice, ministering almost every weekend, my phone constantly ringing with prayer requests, and people needing deliverance, my body was worn out completely. I knew I could not continue to work full-time and minister effectively.

Since I had promised the Lord if He would heal me of the brain tumor and make me every whit whole, I would not just sing and testify any more. but preach the Gospel. I had been unwilling to preach before. I was more confident singing than speaking, because I was embarrassed of my accent. I thought no one would want to hear an orator like me. Nevertheless, I read in the Bible where Paul stated that he did not come "*with enticing words of man's wisdom, but in demonstration of the Spirit and of power*" (1 Corinthians 2:104). Another thought came to me concerning the Lord using a donkey to speak. I assumed if He could use a donkey, He could probably use me , and my mind was at rest.

After returning home from the glorious crusade, I immediately called Brother Love, a great prophet full of wisdom and my dear mentor. I told him of the vision and asked him what to do about it. Did I need to give my letter of resignation to my employer on the following Monday? He suggested that I should wait until I had the faith of God, for He would fulfill my request. A few weeks later, the faith came and my spirit was quickened. It was time to give a letter of resignation and put my hands to the plow and never look back. I quit my full-time job and the journey began.

Another miracle. What an awesome God!

11

Gerald Leaves and My Heart Is Broken

I came home one evening after running errands and as I walked in the door, I could feel that something just was not right. As I turned the light on, I noticed all the music equipment gone and then realized Gerald's clothes missing also. Finding a letter he had written to me, my heart was crushed as I read it and cried uncontrollably. I did not know exactly what to do but once again, this crisis put my faith to the test.

Two weeks before Gerald left, I had just given up my full-time job. I had no money in the bank, and now I did not have a piano player. At this point, the only thing I could do was pray and fast. Trusting the Lord with all my heart, I had to hold on to the horns of the altar and not let go. The next day when I took Patrice to school, I cried out unto the Lord in my distress. Unable to stop crying, I was still very sad. Suddenly, I remembered Margaret Black, the lady who saw me on television and had written a letter to me requesting prayer. She told me to contact her any time I needed a piano player, and that it would be an honor to play for me. When I called and reminded her of her offer to play for me, I was also sobbing as I told her that Gerald had left. In the past, I had prayed for her, but now I was calling her for prayer and she was very understanding. She told me not to worry about anything and as long as I needed her, she would be there for me. Since that time, she has continued to assist me, playing as I minister. I will forever be grateful for Margaret and her family and for all their support and love to serve in this ministry.

Considering all things, I still had bills, Patrice's tuition at a Christian school, and private music lessons. I believed that God would provide. I had no money or sense, but a whole lot of faith, as I have quoted on many occasions. I started praying for God to open doors of opportunity to preach, meet the needs of the people, and sustain our family necessities as well. Immediately after prayer, the telephone rang and a precious lady that I met at one of the meetings of Brother Hall asked me to come and minister at her church that night; I was humbled by His faithfulness. God's Spirit was present in that service and His anointing was evident; Patrice sang and played the saxophone and I preached and ministered in the gifts of the Spirit as God willed. The Lord was faithful to meet the needs of the people and provided for us as well.

The Word of God says, "*I have been young, and now I am old; yet have I not seen the righteous forsaken, nor his seed begging bread*" (Psalm 37:25).

Another miracle. What an awesome God!

SECTION V

*Experiences as
an Evangelist*

1

They're Going to Turn the Water Off, Yet I'm On My Way to Israel

After the dreams of a perfect family no longer existed, God, Patrice and I were alone again. In Psalm 18:29 it states, *"For by thee I have run through a troop; and by my God have I leaped over a wall"*. Actually, I felt as though I had run into the troop and fallen over the wall. I was unemployed because I had given up my full-time job so I would have more time to minister to the needs of God's people. I was ministering in small churches and at Women's Aglow meetings as God opened the doors of ministry, and Patrice and I were again living by faith. The Bible says, *"The just shall live by faith"* (Romans 1:17). At times you wish you weren't so "JUST"! All kidding aside, without faith it is impossible to please God.

One day, after I had prepared a meal for Patrice, I told her to eat. I was going to fast and pray, because I had received a termination notice from the water company. I said, "Patrice, we need a financial miracle by five o'clock or they are going to turn the water off." As I previously had experienced so many times, I knew that God is on time, but seldom early. Standing in the middle of the living room, looking up toward Heaven, I reminded God of His promises. Proclaiming that He would supply my need according to His riches in glory, as I continued to pray, I realized the devil had sent demons of discouragement to my home. I was not a lazy person, but if He would not provide money for utilities, then I would get another job. However, I implored Him not to expect me to get up in the late hours of the night and minister deliverance to His people anymore, because my body was not physically able to do both. Even if Patrice and I had to live on the streets, I would serve Him all the days of my life. Then I felt a release in my spirit, knowing that I had touched the throne room of God. I sent Patrice to the mailbox to check the mail and she came back with a letter in her hand. Enclosed was a money order for seventy-five dollars along with a letter requesting prayer from a preacher by the name of Rev. Bob Marcom, whom I had met in Israel the previous year. This was another miracle and a testimony for me to tell.

I was praising God and told Patrice I was leaving to pay the water bill with money left over to buy a few groceries. So, I got in my car and started driving to the bank with one hand on the steering wheel while the other hand was in the air. With tears flowing I was worshiping God and thanking Him for supplying our needs. I suddenly remembered the prophecy that I had received from Brother Hall concerning ministering on the mission field. As my heart felt touched by His faithfulness, I started to weep, confessing to God that I would go on the foreign soil. However, He would have to tell me what country to go to and He would have to finance the way, because I could barely afford to take care of Patrice and me in Kannapolis, North Carolina, much less in another country. A few seconds later when I went into the thrift bread store, the clerk, who was an acquaintance, looked up at me and said, "Sister Patricia, God told me to tell you to go back to Israel." She then told me that God also told her to pay my way, and she handed me a check for twelve hundred dollars! Can you believe that miracle? It never ceases to amaze me, when I consider that all things are possible to them that believe. Not only do I believe it, but I live it also. Literally within minutes, I went from almost having the water disconnected to receiving a direct answer from God about going to foreign soil. I received prophecy to go back to Israel and preach and the finances to pay for it.

After my experience at the thrift bread store (in which I had planned to buy natural bread but received manna from heaven), I had another affirmation of the prophecy. My friend Rebecca Snipes had visited my home with a book entitled *Glory,* by Ruth Heflin. After reading the book, I realized that Sister Heflin was a woman preacher who also believed in miracles, signs and wonders. Moved by what I read, I felt impressed to call her ministry and speak with someone who could give me more information. When I contacted the office, I conveyed after completing the book, I realized that we shared many of the same beliefs. I shared about some of the many miracles God supernaturally gave to Patrice and me. In addition, I told them that I ministered in the Word and at the altar, while my daughter sang and played the saxophone. We were especially desiring to go to Ruth Heflin's church in Israel to minister. They assured us that we were welcome and expressed delight for us to come and minister. So God opened the door and our trip was paid in full. It was a glorious time for Patrice and me. I have a little saying that I use frequently: If it's God's will, it's His bill; if it's your will; it's your bill. There was no question that this was God's will, because He supernaturally provided all the finances needed to accomplish His will.

Another miracle. What an awesome God!

2

Miracle Provision Allowing Me to Preach

As the ministry began to unfold, many miracles continued to sustain Patrice and me. It was at this time that I began to see the favor of God working on my behalf more than ever. "Favor" is a gift of God that enables one to achieve their assignment. Mordecai knew this, and told Esther, "*And who knoweth whether thou art come to the kingdom for such a time as this?*" (Esther 4: 14). Esther rose to the challenge because of her humility and beauty on the inside. She went from being an ordinary young Jewish girl to a favored queen with a heathen king, who mightily ruled the nations and whose kingdom was unparalleled at that time. Her destiny in God sent her to the kingdom for such a time as this to make an impact and save her people from sure death.

A few months after Gerald left, my heart was still poised to remain in full-time ministry, but I was concerned with how we would be supported, since I had committed to never working full time again. I prayed and asked God for guidance regarding this situation. Shortly after, I received a telephone call inviting me to attend a Christmas party. At the party a friend approached me and told he was praying for me. He inquired of the Lord as to how he could help me and felt impressed to offer me part time employment. He asked me if I would be willing to work part time in his company a few days a week. In addition, if I had a revival or mission trip scheduled, I would be allowed time off to minister. This would enable me to minister, hold revivals, and go on mission trips while receiving a steady income as well as insurance benefits.

The favor of the Lord came to me that day in a special way. Proverbs 12:2 states, "*A good man obtaineth favor of the LORD*". His favor in one day was worth all the lifetime of things I had endured. His favor was the immediate endorsement, which opened the precious doors of ministry opportunity without my having to concern myself about how I would be able to provide for our needs. Likewise, for Ruth, the Moabitess, in a single day the "favor" of the Lord changed her destiny. She understood that it was the "handfuls of purpose," the daily small miracles, that sustained her. She gleaned the wheat in the field that no one else wanted. She and her mother-in-law never went hungry. Just like Patrice and I, we would not go without provision, even in the time of famine, because of Boaz, the owner of the field, whose name means, "in Him (God) is strength." Boaz is compared to Jesus, for he had the means to provide. As Boaz observed her faithfulness, her attitude and her thankful heart, it moved him; he told his servants to give her more. She went from being a widow to becoming his covenanted wife, like we by faith become the Bride of Christ. His favor is set upon us to walk in His covering and protection. *"Keep therefore the words of this covenant and do them, that ye may prosper in all that ye do"* (Deuteronomy 29:9).

I knew that Genesis 24:40 was a promise that I could hold onto: *"The LORD, before whom I walk, will send his angel with thee, and prosper thy way."* Although things had been disheartening when Gerald left, God's favor in a day restored my broken heart and enabled me to move forward in greater love and power.

Another miracle. What an awesome God!

3

Challenged in The Pulpit

One night I was ministering in Laurens, South Carolina, holding a New Year's Eve meeting. As the service was coming to an end, I asked if there was anyone in the meeting who had not accepted the Lord Jesus as his or her Lord and Savior. A young man responded by holding his hand up to confront me, "Yes, lady, I'm not saved and you can't prove to me that Jesus Christ is Lord." "Certainly I can," I answered. Surprised by my calm demeanor, he said, "How, lady?" I held up my Bible that I had been preaching from and said, "By this Bible." Mocking me, he sarcastically said, "That Bible does not prove anything to me because men wrote that book." I answered, "That is right. Men wrote the Bible, but they were men that were inspired by the Holy Ghost." I began to explain to him the plan of salvation. He began to open up to me and confessed that he had heard about the blood and the cross all of his life, but no one as of yet had been able to prove to him that Jesus was Lord.

The intensity began to increase as everyone watched in silence, waiting to see what I would say next. It is in times like this that I am so very grateful for the gifts of the Holy Spirit as listed in 1 Corinthians 12, such as the word of knowledge, which many times operates through me as I am ministering to the needs of the people. Most ministers do not like confrontations like this, because they can be stressful, and I would venture to say that most churches would have had him ushered out. I saw him as an inquisitive, but disillusioned, young man who was looking for a legitimate answer like all of us, but afraid to ask because of fear of what people would think. I thank God that the young man asked me, because he was about to meet "the Man" who was going to tell him everything about himself. His destiny and life would be changed forever, just like the woman of ill repute, rejected by all those in the town who came to the well on that eventful day. In the book of John, the fourth chapter tells of the story of a woman looking for love in all the wrong places, but now she would meet Jesus, the perfect Man. Jesus spoke by the word of knowledge to the broken state of her heart, and she perceived that He was a prophet. That encounter caused her to proclaim in the city, *"Come, see a man, which told me all things that ever I did".(* John 4:29).

His questions were not a challenge for the God that I serve and now with my heart consumed with compassion for him, the gift of the word of knowledge began flowing through me. I proceeded to say, "Son, what about those demon spirits you see, on your wall at night? You cannot even sleep, because you are so terrified. Also, concerning your mother's excruciating headaches, they are not caused by a physical ailment, but by the stress you have caused her; she is concerned for you." Astonished, with eyes wide open in amazement, he backed up and said, "Lady, how do you know that?" "Because", I said, "the God of this Bible that I am holding, and the God of Abraham, Isaac, Jacob and Patricia, just told me so." The Bible declares in Mark 13:11, *"But when they shall lead you, and deliver you up, take no thought beforehand what ye shall speak, neither do ye premeditate: but whatsoever shall be given you in that hour, that speak ye: for it is not ye that speak, but the Holy Ghost"*.

He then replied, "Lady, I love this! I have been in boring churches all my life and no one has been able to prove to me that Jesus was real until tonight." I believed that he, like the woman at the well, was looking for love in all the wrong places, through mediums of New Age and free thinking. He sincerely wanted to know why Jesus was greater than all the gods of other religions. I explained to him that many have a "form of godliness," but "deny the power thereof" as referred to in the book of 2 Timothy. He also asked why more churches did not have people like me preaching in them. I told him Jesus was outside knocking trying to get in and they would not let him in, nor do they want to let people with the real power of God in either. It was truly a New Year's Eve celebration for him, as he came up to the altar for prayer. That notable New Year would usher in a true conversion for this young man that would change him for eternity. For the first time in his life, he would now believe beyond the shadow of a shadow of a doubt that Jesus Christ is Lord and be set free.

As Christians, we need to be prepared to answer questions such as these for believers as well as for the unbeliever. We are called to save the world, not the church. I realize that not everyone operates in the gift of the word of knowledge, but we should all however, be prepared to handle hard questions concerning our faith. We are to *"study to show* [ourselves] *approved unto God,"* as 2 Timothy 2:15 states. God's favor and approval will open your heart to express His wisdom as you defend your faith. At the same time, ask God difficult questions and research the Word. He will guide you to be skillful in your response.

The purpose of operating in the gift of the word of knowledge is not just to predict something in somebody's life, but also to disclose something personal that only God and that person would know. The word of knowledge will open the heart and bring a comprehension of how real God is, eventually making the receiver a believer.

Another miracle. What an awesome God!

4

God Sends Angels
to Lock Motel Doors

Do you believe that God would lock a motel room door and it would actually work out for your good? The story keeps unfolding of the many miraculous things God did in my travels, and as you keep reading, you will see how this all happened. One night, while I was preaching in a school auditorium for a week of revival, God supernaturally locked my motel room door.

On the second night of the revival, there was a small group of people who had many needs. I had come to minister in this meeting without any money and really did not know how we would pay the motel bill at the end of the week. However, knowing that they maintained meager incomes, I was challenged in my faith when I had only received a small offering of fifteen dollars the previous night. Determined to be faithful to the Lord and His people, I knew that they needed to hear the Word of God and that God had indeed sent me to them. The Bible says, in Proverbs 14:31, *"He that oppresseth the poor reproacheth his Maker; but he that honoreth him has mercy on the poor"*. Not wanting to ask the people for an offering, let alone oppress them, the Spirit of the Lord began to move on me and I started to prophesy. I declared that if God wanted to give me a free room, He could send an angel to supernaturally change the lock on my motel room, and make the motel manager give me a free night for my inconvenience. I continued to say that if God wanted to, He could miraculously send me money from Heaven, because with God, all things are possible to them that believe. I had not experienced being locked out of that room to that point, but God was prophetically giving me peace and preparing me for what was about to take place.

After the meeting, my piano player, Margaret Black, drove Patrice and me back to our motel room. We got out of her van and tried to put the key in the door, which did not work. Walking to the front desk of the motel, we asked the manager to assist us in getting into our room, because the room key did not work. Attempting to open the door with his master key that also did not work, he assured us that there would be no problem and he would call for the maintenance man, who was unsuccessful as well. Now the manager was getting very frustrated and embarrassed, so he recommended that we go out to eat at the restaurant while he would call for a locksmith. As he continued to apologize, he said he had never had this problem before and was so sorry for any inconvenience. Then he reassured us and said not to worry about anything, for he would take care of the matter. I asked him if this meant that I would get a free room, and he said, "That is exactly what it means." Hence, we took off for the restaurant, shouting the victory, had a great meal, and returned to the motel. The manager was puzzled as he told us that he did not know how to explain this, but the locksmith had to change the whole lock on the door of the room.

When we finally got into our room, I went to get some ice. As I was walking to the ice machine, I looked down and there was money lying on the ground. The prophecy given earlier that night happened exactly as declared. My angel did a good job keeping the motel manager and locksmith busy, and God was faithful to send money from Heaven to give us a little extra spending money. As the old hymn says, God works in a mysterious way, his wonders to perform." "..*We have seen strange things to-day*" (Luke 5:26).

Another miracle. What an awesome God!

5

It's Electrifying

So often, I am amazed to see God move, especially when you least expect it. It is not always in times of great need, or in large services, but it can be in times of just meeting people. You never know what people are really going through. Often, we go in with preconceived ideas or we look on outward circumstances, developing a notion of who they are. A particular incident transformed my thinking when my friend Vera Carver told me about a husband-and-wife ministry team that taught and preached on the power of deliverance and had personally mentored Prophet Shinn. Intrigued by this, my expectancy was great to meet such special people who were so knowledgeable in the field of deliverance and could be very beneficial to equip me in the ministry. So I went to one of the meetings they held every Monday night in their home.

When we arrived at Bill and Rebecca Barger's meeting in Rockwell, North Carolina, some people were already gathered. We introduced ourselves, and I told Rebecca that I had worked with Prophet Shinn and was so excited to be there. I told them, "If there is anything you taught at the meeting that I do not know, then I want to hear your teaching; the more I can learn, the more I can help other people."

As we were sitting there listening to Rebecca, she suddenly looked at me and said, "Sister Patricia, I believe the Lord is giving you a word for us." At the time she addressed me, I had no sensation that God was about to use me nor did anything come to my mind. Usually, I can feel the anointing stir up my spirit, and that enables me to know that the Lord is about to use me. Then all at once the presence of the Lord came upon me and I started to weep. I said, "I did not come here to minister. I came here to be ministered to, but the Lord is giving me a profound word of knowledge." Truly amazed, I began to tell them what I saw. "I see a past due notice written on an electric bill." Everyone stared at me, questioning the validity of my statement, but I just continued as the Lord kept dealing with my spirit. I said, "I see a cutoff notice from the electric company."

Rebecca Barger's husband looked at me, started crying and said, "Sister, now I know you are a woman of God." He had been sitting in a chair which had pockets on the sides, and he had reached into one of the pockets, and pulled out the very bill I had described. Not telling his wife because she would worry, he just had committed it to prayer. I asked how much the electric bill usually was each month and he told me it usually came to approximately one hundred dollars. Moved with compassion, I continued, "Well, I am an evangelist and I have a small ministry, but I am going to pay your electric bill for one year. Tomorrow morning I will go to the electric company and give them six hundred dollars to apply to your account, and as soon as my income tax check comes in, I will pay the other half. That will be one less bill this year that you will have to be concerned with."

Nevertheless, that was not all God wanted me to do that evening. I had just purchased a spectacular gold bracelet for myself that I had wanted for a long time. Compelled of the Lord, I took my new gold bracelet off and gave it to Rebecca. Now she was weeping like her husband, and she exclaimed, "That is the exact bracelet that I wanted. I showed the same bracelet to Bill around Christmas- time, but when he looked at the price, he said, "Yeah, I bet you would!" I told him someday Jesus would give me that bracelet."

After that initial meeting, I received a letter from Rebecca, who currently is president of the Women at the Well in Salisbury, North Carolina. Still in shock about the whole evening, she had no idea about the electric bill. She praised God and stated that I probably saved her husband's life because she would have been very upset as only wives can truly be, and now she continues to look at her elegant bracelet and thank God. Here I went expecting to receive a blessing from God and learn something new about deliverance and I did. Sometimes deliverance comes in the form of a debt satisfied, so I received the greatest blessing of all, the blessing of giving. I could identify in the area of faith regarding finances knowing how stressful that can be. The Word declares, in Proverbs 18:16, that a person's gift will make room for them and bring them before great people. I am humbled and at the same time very honored to have had the awesome opportunity to minister to such great and wonderful people as Bill and Rebecca Barger.

Another miracle. What an awesome God!

6

Look, Mama, She Can Walk!

There are many opportunities during a service for signs, wonders, miracles and consecration to take place, and I consider these to be some of the greatest and most precious moments I experience as a minister. There was a particular meeting in Calhoun Falls, South Carolina, where I was talking about miracles, and that Jesus is the same yesterday, today and forever. Although God did miracles in the times of the Bible, He could and would perform the same kind of miracles today. Challenging people about the choices they make, I told them it was time to sit in the boat or step out and walk on the water; it was time for them to believe for miracles in their lives. Stirring them up, this message had revitalized their faith in Jesus Christ. Their faith was very strong in this small community of Christians. As the air electrified with the power and presence of Almighty God, the atmosphere was ready for the miraculous manifestations to begin. While I was ministering, I noticed a lady sitting in a wheelchair in the first row and knew that she would be one of the people I would pray for that night. Although her need was great, it did not affect my faith. I knew that the God I was preaching about was real and greatly present in that service, ready to save, heal and deliver.

After preaching, I began to sing inspirational songs as Margaret Black, who was at the piano, played softly and the presence of the Lord filled the room. As the invitation came to all who desired a touch from God to come forward, the altar began to fill up. The lady in the wheelchair came, along with many others, to receive a miraculous touch, and I was later to learn that she had only been restricted to the wheelchair for several years. I began to pray for each person individually. Some gave their lives to God, others had emotional problems, and a few needed physical miracles. While I prayed and laid hands on them, most fell under the presence of God, and then I approached the lady in the wheelchair. Although it was evident that she needed a miracle and would probably request that God restore her ability to walk, I asked her what she wanted me to pray. Confirming my expectation, I asked her, "Are you ready to walk, because this is going to take "water-walking faith." She agreed, so I asked two strong-looking men in the church to take her out of the wheelchair and stand her on her feet and support her while I prayed. She stopped me and said, "I am not ready yet." So I replied, "All right, put her back in her chair. I will pray for her later."

While I continued down the line to pray for others, I knew her faith would be encouraged more as she witnessed the other saints being healed, delivered and set free. Now with her hunger stirred and faith elevated to new heights, I went back to her and said, "Sister, do you believe you are ready to walk on the water now?" With that question, she agreed with me in faith. I asked the gentlemen to return once more to help her. While they kept her steady, she held her arms out to me and I took hold of her hands. I then told them to let her go, saying, "Walk with me, Sister." She began to walk toward me as I took a few steps back, then I let go of her hands as she continued towards me with no assistance.

A small boy in the congregation was so excited, he shouted, "Look, Mama. Look. She can walk. She can walk!" The little boy ran straight to the altar and said, "I want to get saved." His mother followed him and I knelt down beside him to have him repeat the sinner's prayer with me. In response to the prayer, the precious little fellow fell under the power of God, while his mother stood there watching him. With tears streaming down her face, she asked if that meant he was saved. Then she committed her life to follow the Lord. Kathryn Kuhlman once said that miracles were for salvation. This testimony proved true that night in a humble little town of faith-filled believers. A precious woman regained her ability to walk on this earth, but more importantly, salvation came and souls were claimed for God. Their footsteps would be ordered of the Lord and while on this earth, they would be witnesses to the amazing, miraculous power of the living God. Even greater yet, someday their feet will walk on streets of gold.

Another miracle. What an awesome God!

7

"I Want to Be Baptized."

It was an incredibly cold, wintry night when I was ministering in a church in a rural community of South Carolina where approximately one hundred people had gathered to attend the revival. After the sermon, I opened the altar to anyone who wanted prayer in his or her life. As the people came forward for prayer, a darling young girl about eleven years old came forward and approached the altar. As she got a little closer, I noticed that her whole body was trembling, but she walked straight up to me and said, "I want to be baptized." Turning to the pastor of the church to ask him if they had a baptistry, he informed me that they usually baptized people in the creek down the road. I told the young girl that it was very cold, but if she was willing, I would also be prepared to brave the wintry weather.

Surprised by my comments, she gazed up at me and responded in all sincerity, "I don't mean that kind of baptism." Looking at her little body trembling under the power of the Holy Spirit, I questioned, "You don't?" With a look of genuineness in her eyes and the power of God resting on her, she stated, "I want to be baptized with the Holy Ghost, with the evidence of speaking in tongues." There was a deep urgency in her voice, which caught my attention, so I felt prompted by the Holy Ghost to ask her if she knew who Kathryn Kuhlman was. After I told her that Kathryn Kuhlman was about her age when the power of God came upon her, I laid my hand on her precious head and prayed for the power of the Holy Spirit to fall upon her, filling her heart and bringing about the evidence of speaking in tongues.

She fell under the power of the anointing that rested on her and began to speak in her heavenly language. I held the microphone down to her so that the audience could hear her words as she worshiped the Lord. The invocation of the presence of Almighty God fell upon the people and all became blessed by the faith of this young child of God. Never ignore the request of a child, for someday that child might be a great evangelist, prophetess or teacher that God uses to touch the lives of millions.

Another miracle. What an awesome God!

8

No Brass in Your Purses

Matthew 10:9

Because of the miracles I had experienced in my life, particularly my miraculous recovery from a brain hemorrhage, I was invited to share my testimony on a local Christian television program. It was a program aired nightly, co-hosted by Joanne Thompson and Pastor Jeff Wood. Gail Aldridge, who was involved in the Women's Aglow of Greenwood, South Carolina, just happened to watch the program the night I gave my testimony. Intrigued by the simplicity of my demeanor and frankness, she called and asked if I would be interested in speaking at their local Women's Aglow meeting. Apparently, she was not accustomed to people being so open with their faith and speaking without hindrance. She told me that as she was watching the program, she was laughing and crying all at the same time.

What can I say? I suppose you can say I have somewhat of a dry personality and many times I am funny even when I do not intend to be. I am normally very timid until you get to know me, so I was answering questions and telling the story the best I knew how. For instance, when I was asked how I could pay my tithes while I was on welfare, I answered emphatically, "I couldn't afford not to pay my tithes. I was living in poverty and had a sick child, but according to the prophet Malachi, God would rebuke the devourer from our finances and our house." Oftentimes, many Christians tend to project that everything is fine when it is not, and they avoid being vulnerable; however, my straightforwardness caught her attention.

A few weeks later, I received an invitation to speak at that particular chapter of Women's Aglow. Gail invited Patrice, Margaret and me to stay at her house, which was an exquisite bed and breakfast inn. I made sure Patrice ate before Margaret arrived at my home, because all I had was seventy-five cents in my purse, and I did not want Patrice to ask to stop and eat or let Margaret know how broke we were. Margaret picked us up and drove to Gail's beautiful home, which was more spectacular than anything I had ever seen, even in a magazine. Gail opened the door and greeted us with a beautiful, welcoming smile, then she led us to our room. She had reserved the best room in the house for me, complete with a Jacuzzi. It was like walking into a picture-perfect world. On the mantel in the room where I was staying was an envelope with my name on it, and inside I found a check for fifty dollars. Not only did I have the opportunity to stay in such a luxurious place, but God was also providing a blessing to me for being there. I did not sleep much that night because I could not stop weeping for joy. The honor Gail showed me as a guest was truly overwhelming. We awoke to a lovely breakfast, and I was greatly strengthened as I went to the meeting that morning.

The ministry of Women's Aglow has a profound impact ministering to women in Word and prayer all over the United States and abroad, and this service was powerful as many women came for prayer for healing and received encouragement by my testimony. Remember, I had seventy-five cents in cash and a check for fifty dollars, but we were invited out for lunch, so we graciously accepted. Many times by my appearance and presentation, people have not perceived that we were in times of great struggle or in need. I believe that when you minister, there should be an element of dignity since you represent the King of kings and you are an ambassador for Him. Especially since I had testified to the many miracles that God had performed for me, I certainly did not want to ask for money and embarrass myself. One of the officers from the Women's Aglow gave me an envelope when we were leaving, which had a check for one hundred dollars, so now I had one hundred and fifty dollars in checks and seventy-five cents in change.

Margaret had arranged for me to speak to a small congregation in Clinton, South Carolina, the next day and suggested that we just stay over and get a hotel room. I responded that that was fine, but inside my heart was pounding as we drove up to the hotel. I felt as if I was going to break out in a sweat with butterflies in my stomach. As Margaret pulled into the parking lot, she said she felt led to pay for our room, but I heard myself say, "Oh, no, you do not have to do that." What was I thinking? What was I going to give them? Could I rip off half of a check and give it to them or maybe the room would only be seventy-five cents? Oh, Lord, what did I just do? This was very early in my ministry, so totally relying on the Lord progressively gets easier with experience. Thankfully, Margaret insisted and she even gave Patrice and me some money to buy snacks. The money I had received from the ministry and offerings was a provision from God to use to pay my bills and buy groceries when I returned home. It could not have been timelier.

The Word of God declares, in Matthew 10:9, *"Provide neither gold, nor silver, nor brass in your purses."* It was not a problem for me to obey that scripture because I did not have any silver or gold anyway.

Another miracle. What an awesome God!

9

A Little Oil Goes a Long Way

While enjoying a much-needed day off, I was preparing for a mission trip to Jamaica when a dear friend of mine, Celeste, came to the door. When I opened the door, she was visibly upset. She was anxious and talking very fast. It was like someone had put her on fast-forward as she told me about her friend Aileen Auten, who was in need of prayer. According to the doctor, Aileen would require surgery to repair a blockage in her kidney in addition to an aneurysm in her stomach. Celeste urged me to go right then with her to Aileen's house and pray for her to receive her miracle. I said, "Give me time to get ready." Wearily, I started to get ready to go. However, if there was ever a day when I really needed rest, it was that day. Before I left, I took hold of a small bottle of oil that had been prayed over and anointed. As we drove to Mount Pleasant, Celeste asked me if I thought her friend would really be healed. Annoyed by her question, I responded, "Celeste, do you really think, knowing how I feel today, that I would have bothered to even get dressed and go if I thought she would not be healed?" I said, "Of course, I believe she will be healed."

When we arrived at Aileen's home, we rang the doorbell and a precious little lady opened the door with a big smile on her face and a look of expectation. She invited us to sit down after Celeste introduced us to one another, and we began to talk for a while. The dear lady told us that she did not want to have surgery because her mother was in a nursing home and she was concerned that no one would care for her mother the way she did. Consumed with compassion for this little lady, I began to cry as I felt her pain. I asked her if I could pray for her. Taking out the bottle of oil, I proceeded to ask her if she was familiar with the scripture in James 5:14 that states, *"Is any sick among you? let him call for the elders of the church; and let them pray over him, anointing him with oil in the name of the Lord"*. I continued to explain that the oil represented the Holy Spirit and that the power of the Holy Spirit was present that day to heal her. After she gave me permission to pray for her, I touched my hand to the bottle to allow a few drops of oil to fall onto my hands. Laying hands on her, I anointed her with oil and believed without any wavering that she would be healed.

A few days later, I answered the telephone and heard a lady shouting on the other end of the line. The voice was so loud that I had to hold the phone away from my ear to identify who she was. It was Aileen Auten was on the other end making a triumphant proclamation to the highest heavens that she had just received her miracle! She had recently come from the doctor's office, where she had heard the wonderful news that the blockage and the aneurysm were both gone! She continued to expound about how her doctor came into the room bewildered after viewing her new x-rays. He informed her that he did not know exactly what had happened, but she would not need surgery now. He admitted that her prayers must have touched Heaven, since there was nothing wrong with her now and even he was acknowledging a divine intervention, giving the praise to God. Aileen indicated that she believed she was healed because of the oil since she had never been anointed with oil before. The power was not in the oil, but rather in the power of God. Anointing someone with oil is an act of obedience and faith, which is in accordance with the instructions of the Word of God found in the book of James; but Jesus Christ is the Great Physician and healer!

Another Miracle—What an Awesome God!

10

Anointed Wheels

The challenges of being a single parent are continuous. I was always looking for ways to make additional income to keep Patrice in Christian school, give her the best of clothes, and make sure her music education and instruments were the finest. My friend, Evangelist Jerry Christy, who worked at the Hilbish Ford dealership in Kannapolis, North Carolina, would buy used cars, have them repaired, and resell them for extra money. One day when I was talking to him, I had a brilliant idea about a way we could both earn some quick income. I told him I would be receiving extra money from a tax refund and was interested in making an investment with him to split the profit. Thinking it was a good idea, he found a prospective car, which we bought together. However, a year later the car still did not sell.

One day after an important meeting Patrice said, " Mother, let's go out and eat." I was broke that particular day, and also I had always fasted on Fridays. I started to tell Patrice that I didn't have the money to eat out and suggested that we go home so I would fix her something to eat. Suddenly the Lord spoke to my spirit, and told me to break the fast. It was unusual for me to steer away from fasting, because I have always lived a fasting lifestyle, and setting this day of the week as my day to fast. Nevertheless, I told Patrice I felt impressed in my spirit to take her to the Townhouse Restaurant, break my fast, and encouraged her to order anything she wanted, even though I had no money. That had never stopped me before, so why should it now? By now, you know my favorite saying "God's on time but seldom early". We both went into the restaurant and ordered everything we wanted. (Even though we were both very thin, we have always been very big eaters and anyone who knows us knows that is true.) There we both sat with a table full of food with no money to pay for it. Are you wondering how the bill was paid? Just keep reading and you will find out.

About the time we were finished eating, my friend Brother Jerry Christy whom I had not seen for months walked into the restaurant. I greeted him and invited him to sit down to eat with us. When he joined us, I asked about the status of the car. "Why hasn't the car been sold?" He replied, "I don't know." Then he started to preach to me about the principles of paying tithes, giving offerings, and quoting scriptures. As he was sharing his beliefs, I was thinking that I have always paid tithes, given offerings, and could preach that sermon far better than he could. I wanted to put my faith into action because I did not have time to listen to him preach; all I wanted to do was see the car sold. Here I sat while he was preaching, a mother without any money. I needed groceries, and this restaurant bill needed to be paid. I started getting frustrated as I listened to him continue to preach, and if any of you know me, you know it takes a lot to frustrate me. Normally, I am a very patient person, but I finally interrupted him and said, " Brother Jerry, I need money and I need it today. You tell me where that car is parked, and I promise you, as a good mother and a woman of God, I will go and anoint those wheels with a little bottle of oil that I have at home. God will have that car sold today." After learning where the car was located, I immediately stood to my feet to leave and he said, "Give me that bill, Sister. I feel led to pay that today." I said, "You do?" Actually, I really didn't have a plan on how I was going to pay the bill. I was just so focused on getting to the car to pray.

Well, praise God, God always has a plan and a perfect time. If you will obey, He will direct your steps as He did for me that day I went to the restaurant. What if that day I would have said "No" to God? As a rule, I would have thought that fasting was the right thing to do since it was my day to fast. I was to discover that flexibility is vital when you are in the service of the Lord. When Patrice and I drove home, I found my little bottle of oil and went to the Hilbish Ford parking lot. I told Patrice, "Watch this." Kneeling on the parking lot, I anointed every wheel and prayed, "Father God, in the name of Jesus, You said in Your Word, in Philippians 4:19, *"But my God shall supply all your need according to his riches in glory by Christ Jesus."* "Lord, I need groceries for the week. I need this car to be sold today, and I pray that whoever buys this car will never have a wreck in it and it will be a blessing to them." After I prayed and anointed all the wheels individually, I got up, and said, "Come on, Patrice, let's go." Suddenly, Brother Jerry Christy came running out to the parking lot, saying, "Sister Patricia, there is a lady inside my office who wants to buy the car. She made an offer for us to consider. Do you want to sell it?" Thanking the Lord for His faithfulness, I enthusiastically said, "YES. Praise God!"

Because of the passion I have regarding the nature and character of faith, I have little forbearance with people who don't activate their faith in God. Many times they are offended when their lack of faith is challenged or when they doubt those who operate in the "gift of faith." Faith is never offended, but pursues God with a passion and straightforwardness like that of the Syrophoenician woman, in Matthew 15:22-28, who came to Jesus to ask Him for her daughter's deliverance; her faith was tested when Jesus ignored her request at first, and then later compared her to the dogs. That did not stop her from worshiping Jesus. And she came back with the boldness to say that it was true, but even dogs get crumbs. This captured Jesus' attention, and He declared, *"Great is thy faith,"* and her prayer was answered immediately. Faith is being on a mission to capture the heart of God, and, as Hebrews 11:6 states, *"But without faith it is impossible to please him: for he that cometh to God must believe that he is, and that he is a rewarder of them that diligently seek him."* James 1:6-7 says, *"But let him ask in faith, nothing wavering. For he that wavereth is like a wave of the sea driven with the wind and tossed. For let not that man think that he shall receive any thing of the Lord"*.

Patrice and I paid our tithes first and then went to the grocery store and had plenty of money left over. Like the Syrophoenician mother who had great faith, do not ever underestimate the faith of a little praying mother with a bottle of anointing oil.

Another miracle. What an awesome God!

SECTION VI

*A Rare Rose
Comes Forth*

Patrice Receives a Visitation From the Lord

Patrice experienced a visitation from God when she was twelve years old. While I was cooking dinner one day, she had been in her room listening to worship music. Emerging from her bedroom into the kitchen, she said, "Mother, I know one thing about the Lord. He does not need doors or windows and He just walks through my walls." I said, "He does?" She continued, "Jesus came into my room and I saw the nail scars in His hands! He told me to fear not, and never be concerned regarding provision again, because He would always provide for me."

Reminded of this encounter one day when someone called asking for prayer to receive a financial miracle, I prayed in agreement for the miracle to be released. After I hung up the telephone, I prayed and told God that I had needs also, and began to pray for His provision. Notwithstanding, I had prayed with everyone else and their miracles came, but I was on my own at the time and swimming in bills as well. I especially wanted Patrice to be able to continue attending Christian school. Years before, while living in the housing project, I had claimed and believed that Jesus would provide Christian schooling for her. I remember one day holding Patrice as a baby and asking the Lord to make a way for her to attend Christian school by the time she was old enough to attend junior high school, and then graduate from high school. I asked Him this, not for my own glory, but for His glory. I knew Patrice was a front-line soldier in the Kingdom of God. Going to a Christian high school was important to enable her to learn the ways of God in a greater dimension, especially because of her call to the ministry.

As the familiar old song "Operator Information, Give Me Jesus on the Line" mentions, well, Jesus put a minister on the telephone and gave me an answer from God. When I answered the telephone, the man on the other end told me that he and his wife felt compelled of the Spirit to give me a call. He told me that he and his wife watched me in revivals and tent meetings, and noticed that I always gave offerings. Many times, they were aware that I was giving my very last cent. They felt that God wanted to bless and deliver me from debt. He told me to total up all of my outstanding debts and call him back with the full amount. When I mentioned that school was about to start and that I would need to remit a payment, he told me to include the full year's tuition in the balance as well, not just a month's! All my bills including the full year's tuition would come to a total of seven thousand five hundred dollars. Once I called him back, I felt timid and a little ashamed of my debt, but there was no problem, because he gave me the complete amount. The day I received the money, I was glad I had been banking at the First Bank of Heaven. I had made many heavenly deposits that only God knew about and how much I had given. But today was the day for me to make a heavenly withdrawal. By faith, I had given when God laid it on my heart, and had shown myself faithful; God rewarded me. Patrice's vision of Jesus and the words of the prophecy rang true. He always provided for her, and now her full year's tuition was paid in advance. He had released me from all of my debts up to that date. The first thing I did was to pay my tithes on my blessing, and then I paid the full tuition for her senior year. Throughout all the other years, I paid fees month by month, but now it was an unbelievable relief not to be concerned each month for the tuition; now the debt was satisfied before school began. I believe it was important to God that she remain under His wing and under the direction of Christian leadership.

He spoke to His daughter and kept His word and Patrice made an impact in school as a role model and key leader, winning many awards. Her graduation was a significant chapter in her life as she wrote the theme song and gave the graduation speech for the class of 1996. In her very own words, she began to determine her aspirations.

Another miracle. What an awesome God!

A Graduation Speech
by Patrice Renêe Harrold

First and foremost, I would like to thank God and His Son, Jesus Christ, most of all for the many blessings He has given me. One of those blessings happens to be Truth Temple Christian School. I am thankful and count myself blessed to sit under the instruction of Mrs. Howard, Brother Bost and all of my other teachers. I love you all and will never forget the instruction that you have given me. Thank you, Mother, from the bottom of my heart. I love you. Thank you for your many sacrifices to provide me a Christian education and for encouraging me to pursue my goals in music. Proverbs 22:6 declares, *"Train up a child in the way he should go: and when he is old, he will not depart from it."*

Now that you have trained me right, Mom, I can be like King David in Psalm 119:11: *"Thy word have I hid in mine heart, that I might not sin against thee."* At this time I would like to give special recognition to Pastor Garland Faw for having the vision to start TTCS. The Bible says, in Proverbs 29:18, *"Where there is no vision, the people perish,"* and without Pastor Faw this graduating class of 1996 would have never been possible. In conclusion, my prayer is that God will use me in the music field not for mine but for His glory.

Thank you.
Patrice Renêe Harrold

School Song
by Patrice Harrold

Chorus
We want to share this special moment with you.
We want to fulfill the work God has called us to do.
He will lead us all, and with Him
We will never fall.
We will be faithful to His call.

Verse
At times our class may have failed to do everything right.
But we trust in Jesus and the power of His might.
He has made us strong, and will never lead us wrong.
That's why we love to sing our class song.

Verse
This is our prayer:
That God will guide us with His tender
Love and care,
He will not make our road too hard to bear,
So we won't fear,
For '96 is our graduation year.

Bridge
When we put on our caps and gowns,
We will smile and not frown.

2

Patrice Suffers From Depression

Patrice was always full of life and zeal for the Lord. When she was only six-years old, she was singing special solos in churches and at Full Gospel Business Men's meetings. By the time she was ten years of age, she sang for Jim and Tammy Bakker. Patrice also landed the starring role of Imogene Herdman with a local theatre company for their Christmas production, *The Best Christmas Pageant Ever.* After making several appearances on television, Patrice was also granted the honor of singing the national anthem at the Charlotte Coliseum for a Charlotte Hornets basketball game; as fulfilled by the prophetic dream given to me.

It seemed that Patrice was born a shining star. It did not seem to matter what she was involved in; she always became the leading light. Patrice had many accomplishments at a very early age, but her greatest personal accomplishment was winning the Christian Character Award as a senior in high school. Even if Patrice had been a "normal" child, this would have been exceptional. Nonetheless, taking into account that Patrice was born with obstacles set before her, she hurdled them all with grace and dignity. She loved singing so much that as soon as she would get home from school, she would turn on the television, watch PTL, and sing along with the singers. Afterwards, she would go to her room to study the Bible and practice her music lessons for hours. That was her life; she was an effervescent, bright, and happy child.

When she was at the tender age of sixteen, I began to notice a drastic change in Patrice. Her beautiful smile somehow started fading until it almost disappeared, as if someone had let the air out of her. She would go into the bathroom, lock the door, and cry and I would hear her through the door. I could not understand why she was so sad and anxious. Patrice and I were as close as any mother and daughter could possibly be. We would talk together and I would try to comfort her. I let her know she had a mother who loved her dearly encouraging her to always be open with me so that I could help her.

I remember on many occasions talking to her and saying, "I know something is bothering you and it is not normal for you to be sad. You have every reason to be happy; you are a very anointed, extremely beautiful and talented young lady. Most people with your beauty and talent would be conceited and think they were on top of the world." Even though Patrice seemed to have everything going for her, she was always down on herself. She began to suffer anxiety attacks, slept a lot, and lost interest in practicing her music. I knew this behavior was not normal for Patrice, so I became very concerned. I started seeking God, and at the time, I could only tell God and a few close friends about the pain that Patrice and I were going through.

One night as I was sleeping, Patrice came into my bedroom and woke me up, saying, "Mother, you have been hurt more than anyone I know, but if I do not tell you this, I will never be able to sleep again." Crying uncontrollably, her little body trembled as she began to pour out her heart and share secrets with me that she had held for years. I held her as tight as I could to let her know that she had some security. I told her I loved her, next to the Lord, more than anything or anyone, and that I would help her through this trial. After talking with her that evening, this was the beginning of healing for the wounds she had, which would take years to mend.

At the time Patrice was going through this, I was teaching a Bible study at a local church and I was supposed to be the one with all the answers. Patrice had been playing music and singing for many evangelists, churches, revivals and weddings. Though many people knew us, they did not understand. Unfortunately, Patrice and I suffered a lot of persecution having false accusations spoken, as well as much heartache. It was almost too much for one to bear, so you can imagine how difficult it was for a sixteen-year-old girl, who had never hurt anyone. She was the most dedicated Christian I had ever known, and anytime anyone needed prayer, she was the first one to pray for them. She had a heart of gold, with much compassion for God's people. I was determined that Patrice would overcome the depression and being the happy, beautiful and vivacious girl she had once been.

3

Get Dressed, We're Going Shopping!

I will never forget how Patrice suffered from depression after all she had been through and I tried everything I knew to make her happy. As a single parent, my finances were limited, but I never really lived on a budget, as most people would in my situation. Then again, my way of thinking is different from most people's way of thinking because, as you know by now, God has given me "the gift of "faith." The Word of God declares, in Mark 11:24, *"What things soever ye desire, when ye pray, believe that ye receive them, and ye shall have them"*. I felt Jesus was the only Father and husband Patrice and I had. After all, the Word of God declares, in Isaiah 54:5, *"For thy Maker is thine husband; The LORD of hosts is his name; and thy Redeemer the Holy One of Israel; The God of the whole earth shall he be called"*. When I wanted something, I would just make my petition known to Jesus, my Provider, who is the King of kings.

I remember it was a sunny day, but Patrice looked sad, so I said, "Patrice, get dressed, we're going shopping! I am going to buy you a whole new wardrobe." She loved to shop, so I thought that would make her happy, except her response was, "Mother, we don't have any money." Patrice was more practical than I am. However, I never let a little thing like money stop me from shopping. I knew in my spirit that God would make a way. After getting dressed, we got into the car ready to pull out of the driveway, when suddenly, a friend drove up beside me and said, "I have a card for you, but please don't open it until I leave." After my friend left, I told Patrice to open it and read it. She exclaimed, "Mother, there is a check for one thousand dollars in here!" I said, "Let me see that." Sure enough, there was a check for one thousand dollars in my hand, and with that blessing, Patrice and I were able to go shopping and eat dinner too; we had a wonderful day. The Lord really does supply all our needs, but also delights to give us the desires of our hearts.

Another miracle. What an awesome God!

4

Patrice and I Experience the Glory

My friend Rebecca Snipes came to visit me and told me about Ruth Heflin's glorious camp meetings held in Ashland, Virginia, where miracles, signs, and wonders were taking place. Excited about going and experiencing the move of God for myself, I told some other friends about it, and we decided to load a van full of hungry Christians. Off we went to Ashland to experience the awesome glory of God.

When we arrived at the meeting, I had never seen anything like it from the moment the service began. Jane Lowder, part of the ministry team and an anointed woman of God, started inviting people to come to the front and dance before the Lord. The service intensified as she exhorted and people worshiped. As the musicians played, people started running to the altar dancing unto the Lord. Patrice and I joined in, and felt such freedom to worship as we both danced before the Lord. His presence was so real that it felt as though we had left earth and ascended into Heaven into the very throne room of God. The very air seemed charged with the breath of God. Those meetings are where Patrice and I learned the importance of dancing before the Lord; we learned we could dance our way to victory. Psalm 30:11 declares, *"Thou hast turned for me my mourning into dancing: thou hast put off my sackcloth, and girded me with gladness."* The next time we visited the camp meeting, Patrice took her saxophone and played while I danced.

Books written by the prophetess, Ruth Heflin were available at the campground, so Patrice and I bought several books to read. I had never seen a woman of God so anointed as Ruth Heflin, moreover, I knew she had something that we needed and wanted. When we got home from the camp meeting, we were so excited to read about how she danced before the Lord every day. Even when she was traveling on airplanes, she would go in the bathroom and leap up and down.

Patrice and I were inspired to dance before the Lord daily, and since that time, danced every day before the Lord.

We called Brother Love and told him about dancing before the Lord as part of our daily praise and worship, which pleased him greatly. Even though Patrice was still fighting depression, it was not nearly as bad as it had been in the past. Sometimes she would be so depressed she would just sit in a chair, looking lifeless, and say, "Mother, I just feel like giving up. What's the use?" I would take her by the hand and say, " Come on, Patrice, we're going to dance before the Lord." Psalm 149:3 declares, *"Let them praise his name in the dance: let them sing praises unto him with the timbrel and harp."* As I would dance with Patrice, I would sing different prophetic utterances, such as, " Miracles, signs and wonders tonight, Patrice is going to make it in the worship band. Patrice is beautiful, talented, anointed and she can do all things through Christ who strengthens her." We would sing before God until the glory of the Lord would come upon us, and every bit of that depression would leave. Patrice loved the worship songs she learned at the camp meeting so well that she began to sit down at the piano and play all of them. I would sing and dance for hours with her and the glory of God would fill the whole house.

Often as people would come to our house, Patrice would play the piano and sing the beautiful chorus "You Deserve the Glory." Our guests would be greatly touched by her melodious praise, conveying how they could feel the presence of a thousand angels when she sang that glorious song. Every day Patrice was coming closer and closer to victory over depression, so I will always be grateful for the influence and ministry of Ruth Heflin. It was experiencing the glory of God in those meetings that taught me how to help my daughter get the deliverance she needed, and to become the overcomer that I knew she was.

Another miracle. What an awesome God!

5

Patrice's Trip to the Bahamas

Reverend Darrell Bragg and Reverend Peggy Poppy asked Patrice if she would like to go with them to the Bahamas on a short term mission's trip to sing and play the piano for the services they would hold. Patrice was so excited as they drove to Fort Lauderdale, Florida, and then boarded a cruise ship for the Bahamas. At the time, Patrice did not know Sister Poppy very well, but they became fast friends as they shared a room in the Bahamas. She grew to know that Sister Poppy was a woman of great faith, and Brother Darrell kept Patrice in stitches with his witty personality that she loved so dearly.

However, this was not a pleasure trip where they had the opportunity to enjoy the beach and visit the tourist attractions of the islands. They would spend their time in the mainland areas stricken with poverty. When she was a little girl, Patrice used to quote this scripture: *"And he said unto them, Go ye into all the world, and preach the gospel to every creature"* (Mark 16:15). Patrice was happiest when she was ministering in some capacity, whether it was singing, playing an instrument or witnessing for the Lord. At twenty-one, Patrice had lived out a dream that she had had all her life, as she was finally able to reach out with the love of God in a different part of the world. Brother Darrell shared with me that she conducted herself on the entire trip as a light for God. That trip transformed her understanding, as she experienced the power of God praying for salvation and healing among foreign people. Most young people would dream of going to the islands to lie on the beach and enjoy the pleasures of the islands, but Patrice's dream was to take Jesus to the islands and she spent this trip living out her dream.

When a young person goes on a mission trip, leaving the familiarity of their immediate surroundings, it gives them an understanding of different cultures and lifestyles. Most of all, it enlightens them to begin to see just how much God loves all nations, the people of every tongue and creed. They come back with a new appreciation of the scripture that says, *"For God so loved the world, that he gave his only begotten Son"*. (John 3:16). They are forever impacted as revival fires burst forth in their hearts, to witness and to be a witness. I would encourage parents to allow young people to experience these types of mission trips as often as they can. It will open their hearts, and birth within them the compassion to bring hope to the lost souls of the nations.

Another miracle. What an awesome God!

6

It's Off to Nursing School

One morning while Patrice and I were talking, she asked if I had any ideas about what she could do with her life in addition to her musical pursuits, and so I committed to prayer for clarity of direction to be given to her for her life. In Proverbs 3:5-6, we are admonished: *"Trust in the LORD with all thine heart; and lean not unto thine own understanding. In all thy ways acknowledge him, and he shall direct thy paths"*. God is concerned and wants to be involved in every aspect of our lives from ministry to occupation, to where we live and the things we are apprehensive about, and it is our privilege to seek His face and find His counsel for our lives.

After praying in all earnestness for my daughter's direction and knowing how kind and big-hearted she was, I suggested that she would make a wonderful nurse. This would be a way to establish a career directed at helping people while continuing to develop her music ministry. Elaborating further, I suggested that she start with the community college program for nursing, and then continue taking classes after graduating to become a registered nurse. Later that same day, God confirmed our conversation during her counseling session when her therapist suggested the exact same thing. He said, "Patrice, I believe you would make an excellent nurse." Proverbs 11:14 states, *"in the multitude of counselors there is safety"*. Excited, she exclaimed, "That was the same thing my mother just told me!" Confident knowing that this was God's will and direction, Patrice and I immediately began looking into the programs that were available to her.

Before we approached the Employment Security office, we prayed, sang and danced before the Lord. We asked the Lord to help us find favor with those who would have the authority to release the funds needed for Patrice's education. When we arrived at the office, we spoke with a supervisor who had the authority to make or break this new aspiration. Or so she thought, but we knew that God was in control. At first, she seemed cold and distant while questioning Patrice. She even told Patrice that she did not feel like she was sincere in her desire to go to nursing school. I stood inside the door with all of the righteous indignation a mother feels when her child is being attacked and just prayed. As I continued to pray, I looked at Patrice and literally saw the miraculous golden glory of God visible on Patrice's face. Then I knew that my prayer had touched the throne room of God. God began to fill Patrice with words of wisdom and sincere appeal. As the lady listened to her, her countenance changed, then her heart softened. Proverbs 3:4 states: *"So shalt thou find favor and good understanding in the sight of God and man"*. When Patrice found favor with God and man, suddenly the lady reconsidered Patrice's options and felt she would be able to help her pursue her professional goals. Not only would they cover her full tuition, but also her books, uniforms and supplies.

With hearts full of gratitude that God had given us favor, we soon went to shop for her uniforms and the first book needed for her curriculum. Within two days, Patrice had read and studied the entire book.. She completed the requirements for Certified Nursing Assistant certificate, graduating with honors, she continued her education at Rowan Community College while working at Big Elm Nursing Home in Kannapolis, North Carolina.

The patients loved Patrice and she loved them. During her breaks, she would play the piano and sing songs of worship for the patients. My little rose bud was opening up, and the fragrance of her life was becoming evident as she grew into elegance, independence and self-sufficiency. It gave her much joy and contentment to help people, and loved it when the patients would tell her that they missed her when she took a day off. The blessing that she received in helping others was a great reward and God was giving to her a new approach to life and adulthood. As Patrice helped others, God was helping Patrice overcome her anxieties, fears and depression.

Another miracle. What an awesome God!

7

Brother Darrell, I Have Never Kissed a Boy Before

It was around February of 1999, when Patrice and I went to a little town in South Carolina to minister in a revival. My little girl was beginning to flourish in more ways than one. Her big, beautiful clear blue eyes, petite stature and long, flowing blond hair made her stand out among all the fair maidens in the land. She was my little storybook princess just waiting for that wonderful Prince Charming to sweep her off her feet. Since Valentine's Day was approaching, Patrice was starting to wonder what it would be like to fall in love. She had kept so focused on her walk with God, academics and music that she had limited social interaction. My heart was filled with compassion when I considered the challenges she faced as a young lady who was living a life of holiness. I knew that it was a bit overwhelming for her tender heart.

It is at that time in your life when all of a sudden, you want to be grown up and yet remain a child. It is a time of many recurring questions, such as: What do You want me to do for you, Lord, and how do I accomplish what it is that you want me to do? What are Your priorities, and how do I balance my desires? I was thankful for Brother Darrell Bragg, who was like a big brother to Patrice. She trusted him, so one night after the service, Patrice pulled him aside in her frustration and exclaimed, "Brother Darrell, is there something wrong with me? Am I not pretty or something? I have never even had a boyfriend or a kiss!" Brother Darrell said, "Patrice, you are a very beautiful girl! There is nothing wrong with you! The Lord has put a hedge of protection around you because you have a great anointing in your life. Someday you will get your kiss, I assure you."

Brother Darrell began to minister to her as he shared the story of Ruth and

Boaz with Patrice. Boaz had commanded the men who worked in his fields to respect Ruth and to leave her alone. Ruth 2:15 *"Let her glean even among the sheaves, and reproach her not"* (Ruth 2:15). He explained that God had commanded the young men around her to respect her in order to keep her from hurt and harm. Patrice indeed was my little "Ruth", faithfully following me from meeting to meeting. She was faithful to seek the Lord, and get her portion of the "handfuls of purpose" from God. I began to commit her ways to the Lord, that God would keep her safe. For the time being, however, Brother Darrell's support and words of encouragement seemed to comfort Patrice. She knew she was special, and that God had a specific plan for her life.

Another miracle. What an awesome God!

8

Patrice Wins a Beauty Pageant

When Patrice was about four, I called her father and asked if he would like to help me pay for an Easter dress for her to wear to church. He said no, he had a beautiful daughter now, but he was not referring to Patrice. The other girl was the daughter of the woman with whom he was living, who would someday win a beauty pageant. I agreed that the little girl was a beautiful child; nevertheless, I prophesied that Patrice would be a beautiful young lady as well. She would also be anointed to sing and play music all over the world. He replied angrily back at me, "Patty, why don't you quit living in a dream world? Those short, stubby little fingers would never play an instrument." I was devastated by his remark, and could not believe that he would say such a thing about his own daughter. Patrice was not a "pretty" baby like most normal children. Her squinty eyes, swollen hands and feet, webbed neck, and prognosis of being short in stature, made her future as a famous musician unpromising. Nonetheless, a beauty queen seemed even more unlikely.

No one ever made comments that she was a beautiful baby or a pretty little girl except her Aunt Pam, who said when she was born that she looked like a beautiful little rosebud. Since her father was not a Christian, he looked at the diagnosis with all of its assumptions. But I looked to God. He believed the doctor's report, but I believed the report of the Lord. He made it clear that he was not interested in buying her the Easter dress or doing anything for her. He was right, I did live in a dream world, because I knew God was the author of my dreams and all His dreams come true. Jeremiah 23:28 states, "*The prophet that hath a dream, let him tell a dream; and he that hath my word, let him speak my word faithfully.*" To this day, all the dreams that God has ever given me have always come true. Remembering those former moments that challenged my faith, I felt compelled to write this story of how God's promise came to pass. My transformed daughter entered a beauty pageant, something she would never have dreamed of. "But God" penned the story and this "rare rose" was about to blossom.

When Patrice was about twenty-two years old, I was working with someone who was involved with beauty pageants. She suggested I ask Patrice if she would be interested in entering a pageant. When I asked her, she was interested, so we had a lot to do in a short time to get ready, especially since we were not familiar with all the details. We were in need of buying the perfect dress and accessories to participate in the evening gown competition. Shopping until we were ready to drop, we went to every store in Salisbury, Kannapolis and Concord, and still could not find the right dress. Patrice was starting to get anxious by four thirty, since the stores would soon close. I reassured Patrice that God's on time, and seldom early, but God was going to help us find that dress right on time. I remembered about a consignment shop in Concord and felt compelled to go there, pulling up ten minutes before they closed the store. As we walked in, Patrice immediately saw a beautiful long blue sequined gown on a mannequin, which looked perfect, so I encouraged her to try it on. What a miracle! It was a perfect size three that fit her as though it was handmade just for her, and we found it right on time.

In her first competition, she won in all the pageant categories, which included Most Talented, for playing a beautiful rendition of "I'd Rather Have Jesus" with the alto sax, the Angel Award, Most Beautiful Eyes, and Miss Congeniality. This greatly encouraged Patrice and gave her self-esteem a much-needed boost. When the opportunity arose to enter another pageant, Patrice enthusiastically entered the competition and was much better prepared. Again, Patrice was the overall winner, not only winning Most Beautiful Eyes, Overall Most Talented, and Best Smile, but also crowned Miss Easter Extravaganza 2000 Queen.

Did this sound possible according to her diagnosis at birth? What if I had given my precious daughter up for adoption as her dad suggested we do shortly after her birth? I would never have experienced the feeling I had that day, watching her as she grew in self-confidence, outshining everyone because of her anointed music and the beauty the Lord had bestowed upon her. It is imperative to speak words of blessings over our children daily. Mark 11:23-24 admonishes us to speak to our mountains of circumstances; we can say to our mountains, "Be removed", and by faith we can have whatsoever we say, not doubting or wavering. When we pray, it is important to believe and call those things that are not as though they are. Despite the circumstances that surrounded Patrice's birth and along with our difficulties and hardships, I spoke in faith, and like Abraham, did not stagger at God's promises that He spoke to my heart. Romans 4:20-21 states:

"He staggered not at the promise of God through unbelief; but was strong in faith, giving glory to God; and being fully persuaded, that what he had promised, he was able also to perform". There was never a doubt in my mind of God's promises concerning Patrice. Every day I would tell her that she was beautiful, talented encouraging her to speak the same to strengthen her faith.

The fact may be that your child may have some type of affliction, but the truth is that by His stripes, we are healed. You can invalidate the plan the enemy has, and speak words of life by faith to change the prediction. As Christians, we choose to walk by faith and not by sight. Knowing that God is no respecter of persons, He will do for your child what He did for mine. Parents, please never give up on your children. Always remember that children are an awe-inspiring gift to us from God. They are true miracles of life that come into our hearts and lives to enrich our day-to-day walk and make us better people. My belief has always been that gifts are to be appreciated and treasured.

Another miracle. What an awesome God!

9

Peter Has a Dream

I received a call one afternoon from an evangelist, James Nemeth, who was preaching in South Carolina. He felt the leading of the Holy Spirit to visit my home and minister at the home meeting. When he returned to his home in Florida, he called telling me that his mother wanted to speak to me. I didn't know her at the time, so he asked if that would be okay, to which I said yes.

Sister Irene began to tell me about another son she had, much younger than James, named Peter, who was working in New York City at the time. Peter had recently called her and said, "Mother, I am getting married." She said, "Congratulations, son, to whom?" He replied, "I don't know her yet, but I know what she looks like. I had a dream of her last night." Sister Irene continued to elaborate of his description of the beautiful young lady in his dream. He told her she had short blonde hair, which was curled under, and had blue eyes. She stood as a very petite lady who was approximately five feet three inches tall. Somewhere between the ages of twenty-one and twenty-two, she was sitting in a tall tree wearing a long blue dress playing an alto saxophone. As he looked up to her, he asked her to marry him, to which she replied, "Okay." "That is the girl I am going to ask to marry me," he said. Katherine, James's daughter traveled with her father and attended our home meeting that night. She was on the other telephone listening to everything Peter said. She got so excited when she heard of the dream, and she said, "Grandma, I know that girl! I met her this weekend! Her name is Patrice, and she is Sister Patricia Thomas' daughter." After I heard the story, I agreed that the description of the girl sounded exactly like Patrice. Peter's mother asked if I would care if her son Peter would call Patrice. I gave my approval for him to contact her, and told his mother, "God gives me many prophetic dreams" and believed that this was a prophetic dream given to Peter by God.

When Peter called Patrice, he described the dream to her and she was quite amazed. They developed a rapport on the telephone, talking frequently, and the time had come when he was interested in meeting her. When his job in New York City was finished, he would go to Florida for a few things and then come to visit her. The day finally arrived when Peter came to our house to meet Patrice. I still remember Patrice anxiously waiting to meet him; she looked exceptionally beautiful that day. The tension mounted as the doorbell rang and Peter finally arrived. I cautiously answered the door because I was very protective of Patrice, wanting to guard the fact that she had lived such a sheltered life and had never even kissed a boy.

When I opened the door and saw Peter, I went into total shock, because he reminded me so much of her biological father. He looked like a typical musician, with long hair and a handlebar mustache. His style of dress was not as conservative as we were accustomed to seeing on a young Christian man. Patrice always said she wanted a person who dressed more like a preacher, a more conservative type with short hair who wore a shirt and tie. Peter absolutely did not fit that description; thus she was in shock, and so was I. Peter stood at the door with a large pink rose and a teddy bear in his hand. As Patrice came down the stairs, Peter handed her the teddy bear. After we all introduced ourselves, they sat on the sofa to talk. Then Peter handed her the beautiful rose with an engagement ring and wedding band attached, which astonished us even more. He told me that he loved her from the time he saw her in the dream. She was the only girl for him and he wanted to marry her.

In the beginning, Patrice being a very out spoken and honest person explained, to Peter that she did not know him well enough, and was not attracted to boys with long hair and handlebar mustaches. As they had the opportunity to know each other better over the weekend, he said he was willing to cut his hair and shave his mustache. She said, "You are such a nice person and I don't want you to change for me. You need to find someone who will like you for who you are." After their initial visit for the weekend, he went back home with a commitment to visit us again.

The next time we saw Peter, he had his hair cut and he was clean-shaven, which was a step in the right direction. Patrice and Peter continued getting acquainted, discovering that they had many common attributes. They loved the Lord, were singers and musicians, playing the saxophone for the glory of God. It appeared that Patrice and Peter were starting to get more serious about each other. Peter was showing her love that I was not able to give her. After all, I loved her with a mother's care, but he was able to love her in a romantic way. One day Peter gave Patrice a ride to work after dating for a few months. He later called me to tell me that Patrice received her first kiss at the tender age of twenty-two. And so, Brother Darrell was right; she did get her kiss.

During this time Patrice was trying to make the right choice about considering marriage as an option or continuing her career pursuits. I deeply appreciated her loyalty and dedication to do only what God wanted her to do. As she prayed and consulted the Lord concerning Peter's proposal, she did not feel it was the proper time to make a commitment. She told Peter that she just wanted to concentrate on her schooling and continue to dedicate her time to practicing her music for the Lord. Patrice's aspirations were not of this world but focused on eternity, and though Peter was a wonderful person, he was an earthly man who was no rival to Patrice's true love, which was Jesus Christ.

Peter's dream did come true, for he met the girl of his dreams, and they continued a loving relationship as friends. However, Patrice's heart had already been spoken for, which you will understand more clearly as the story of our miracle unfolds.

Another miracle. What an awesome God!

10

Mother, What Would You Do if I Got Married

Patrice always concerned herself with what would happen to me if she ever left and got married. It was as if Patrice and I were inseparable. Always together, we made a good team. I would preach and Patrice would sing and play. As we drove to the meetings, Patrice would have a notepad and pen in hand to write the things the Lord put in my spirit to minister about. Looking up scripture references for me, she would have a full outline ready to hand me by the time we arrived at the meeting. She would then choose her songs to reflect and support the theme of the sermon as if we knew exactly what the other was thinking. We were not only a dynamic mother and daughter team, but also best friends who worked together hand in hand.

She knew my life would be challenging and lonely without her, and would often ask, "Mother, what would you do if I got married?" I told her I would do everything to help her when she became a wife, and felt that I had already experienced marriage and lived a good life. I jokingly told her not to concern herself about me, because I could keep my house clean and would not have anyone to pick up after. I was always trying to make her laugh. The message I was trying to convey to her was that if she was happy, then I would be happy too. In essence, whatever choices Patrice would make in her life, I wanted her to know that I would encourage and celebrate them.

I reassured her, "Patrice, I know you have always been saddened because you missed out on the love your real father could give because of his decision to distance himself from you. There are little orphans, who have never had the love of a father or a mother. When I know you are well taken care of, then I would go to the little orphans. I would teach and train in the love of God as I did you, and shower them with the love of a mother. Even though your father was not there for you, you had a mother that loved you enough for a million people. There is not a day that has gone by that you have not heard the words I love you or been hugged and kissed. Those children have never had a mother or a father to show them love so I will impart the love of a mother.

In remembrance of those words when Patrice left, I did not abandon the promise I made her. I do minister to the orphans on foreign soil several times a year, and I love them dearly.

Another Miracle—What an Awesome God!

11

This Time I Made It After All

Patrice heard that Toni Bogart-Syvrud was coming to Kannapolis, North Carolina, to be the music minister at Metro Worship Center, and if Patrice ever had an idol, it was Toni. She thought she was the greatest teacher and singer she had ever heard and really wanted to play saxophone on her worship team. Overwhelmed with excitement, she asked Toni if she could be in the band. Toni explained to her that she, as a music minister, expected an excellent spirit from everyone. Going into detail about the principles of godly leadership, prominent team members would have to attend church faithfully for six months and come to practice every week on time, in addition to practicing daily. Toni's rules seemed to be strict but she demanded the best, and because of her methods, her praise band was astounding. During the months that followed, Patrice did just as Toni had instructed and was faithful to church and practice.

Patrice was still struggling through depression and attending college, but she was determined to be a part of the music at Metro. After six months, Patrice came home unhappy and miserable one night after practice, went to her bedroom and cried. She said she was giving up because Toni was still not going to let her play in the band on Sunday. I tried to console her, but she would say, "I'll never make it and I'm not going back." With her crying uncontrollably, I would say, "Patrice, let's dance," and I would take her by the hand and sing, "Patrice is going to make it in the band." We would both sing and dance as the glory of God would fall on us and Patrice's attitude would change. By the end of the prayer and dancing she would say, "Yes, Mother, you're right." Toni continued to work with Patrice, trying to teach her to be part of the band, and then the time came when it all became worth it. One night after rehearsal, she came home thrilled, "Mother, you can't say that I'm not determined. I was determined to make it Mother!" Then she sang out, "This time I made it after all."

The following Sunday as she played her saxophone, it was so moving, I wish you could have seen her that day as her beautiful hands moved over the keys of the saxophone, one hand raised toward Heaven worshiping her true love. It was the most precious sight I have ever seen. The music that day was incredibly anointed. It felt as if Heaven had descended to the earth and the room was full of God's glory. Brian, Toni's husband, told her that he heard a sound from Heaven, and when he looked up, he saw Patrice glowing as she played. He knew that God had received her worship as a sweet fragrance. Pastor Gary later told me that when he returned home, he received a telephone call commenting on how anointed the worship seemed to be that day. Although they did not know what had changed, it was the most anointed music their church ever experienced. I said, "Pastor Gary, I don't mean to sound like I'm boasting, but I believe the reason the worship service was so intense today was because of the anointing that God bestowed upon my daughter;" Pastor Gary agreed.

Another Miracle—What an awesome God!

12

Christmas in October

Gold Car

The new millennium brought Patrice and me blessings, upon blessings and the year was going by rapidly. Taking into account how faithful God was to bring us through the many hardships we had endured over the previous years, we had prevailed over persecutions, heartaches, trauma and finances. Nevertheless, the year 2000 was different, miraculous doors were opening in ministry, and there was a strong outpouring of the Holy Ghost with miracles, signs and wonders. By January of that year, Patrice turned twenty-two. With her world turning around, she had everything going for her. Of the many wonderful things that happened, Patrice won the beauty pageant, which boosted her self-confidence after her long bout with depression. We also moved into a beautiful new apartment that my friend Carolyn Atwell owned, which was in a great location and close to the church. Carolyn loved Patrice and especially loved to hear her sing or play her saxophone. When Patrice was struggling, I would call a few of my closest friends to fast with me and Carolyn was one of them. She knew of Patrice's struggle with depression, and prayed and fasted many times for her.

My friend Susan who breeds Maltese puppies had a new litter and felt led to give Patrice one of the pups. One thing Patrice always wanted was a puppy, but we had always lived in apartments that did not allow pets. I called Carolyn, explained the situation, and told her that I thought it might cheer Patrice up and bring her further along on her road to recovery. Normally, she did not allow it, but since it was for Patrice, she made an exception. Celeste and I drove to Greensboro to bring the puppy to its new home, and when Patrice came home from work that day, she was overjoyed. "Joshua Caleb" looked like a little toy, and when this tiny bundle of white fluff saw Patrice walk in the door, he ran to her as if he knew instantly that she was his master. He just loved to hear her play the saxophone, piano and flute. A little mischievous as only puppies can be, he knew he was not allowed to go upstairs, so he would sit at the bottom of the steps and wait for the telephone to ring. When I would answer the phone, he thought he would outsmart me and hop right upstairs to join Patrice in her room as she played. He knew instinctively that if I was on the telephone, I would not be able to scold him. So, off he would go, and my frustration would amuse Patrice when I complained about him not minding me. Joshua, our new addition, was a true delight and instrumental in bringing much comfort to Patrice.

As I was on my way one day to pick up Patrice from work, the Spirit of the Lord began to deal with me. When Patrice came, I began to share what God was showing me about giving us a gold car with champagne gold leather seats. At that time, we were only driving a little red Ford Escort. My friend Jerry, who is an evangelist and car salesman, called and told me that he had recently talked to a young man that I knew who was trading his car. He thought it was the perfect car for me. He then described a gold car with champagne gold leather seats and a moon roof that belonged to the youth pastor of the church Patrice and I were attending. I said, "You are not going to believe this, Brother Jerry, but on the way home today I just told Patrice that God was going to give us a car that fit that exact description!" Since they were not able to negotiate a trade, Jerry suggested that I call the owner and speak to him directly. I called and made an offer, but as you already know my motto, I had no money and no sense, but, I had a whole lot of faith and it works every time. After all, why should I let a little thing like money stop me, I never had before. God had already shown me prophetically through the word of knowledge that I was going to get a car just like that. A wise man once said, "You are never as far from a miracle as it first appears." After speaking with the youth pastor, I asked him to prayerfully consider the bid, the following Sunday he told Patrice that he was willing to accept the proposal. I was thrilled and knew that the power of agreement would release the miracle, so I asked Patrice to agree with me in prayer that God would provide the finances needed. The Bible says in Matthew 18:19, *"Again I say unto you, That if two of you shall agree on earth as touching any thing that they shall ask, it shall be done for them of my Father which is in heaven"*. By a miraculous turn of events that day, God supplied the money and the car was paid in full!

Everything was finally looking more encouraging for us, after all we had been through. We were now walking in restoration and blessing. Big Elm Nursing Center employed Patrice on the same day she received her Certified Nursing Assistant certificate. She continued her education in nursing at Rowan Community College while my ministry was taking off and we were traveling to churches all across the United States. It seemed as though Patrice received her full life again as she met Peter, her first boyfriend, and was accepted into the praise band at Metro Worship Center and was gainfully employed all at the same time. God had given us a beautiful gold car with champagne gold leather seats and we were riding the waves of glory with God at the helm; I was delighted to just rest in God's arms.

It was Saturday morning in the second week of October when I entered into a treasured time of prayer and worship. I felt a strong sense about putting the Christmas tree up to celebrate Christmas early that year. I said to Patrice, "God is blessing us so much. It's almost Halloween, and if people can observe that type of holiday, we can certainly celebrate our Lord's birthday." After contemplating God's provision and faithfulness, with my heart full of gratitude, I wanted to honor Him. Patrice and I went shopping to choose a beautiful Christmas arrangement to decorate our living room. None were available that early in the season, so combining our own creative styles, we set out to buy a magnificent assortment of flowers, ribbons and accessories and a candle for the florist to arrange into a lovely Christmas arrangement. I remember Patrice commenting on how expensive it would be, but I responded, "Certainly, but after all He has done for us, nothing is too costly for Him."

We had such a wonderful day and it was just as if we were surrounded by angels all day long. Jade, Patrice's best friend, came over to watch a movie and have snacks, while friends of mine came by for prayer and fellowship. I had prayed earlier for God to send someone to help me put the tree together and decorate it. When my friends came by unexpectedly, I knew God had sent them to help me, which they did following our time of prayer. After everyone left, Patrice was delighted as she saw the elegant tree all lit up in burgundy and gold and the house filled with the fragrance of Christmas. Our tradition was to cuddle up drinking hot chocolate, enjoy the lights on the tree, and meditate on the goodness of God. As we worshiped the Lord in gratitude, reflecting on all the wonderful things He had so richly blessed us with that year, His Presence came and filled the living room. Overwhelmed with joy, I told Patrice that we should drive our new car right through the living room door, park it under the tree, and put a big red bow on it. With a radiant smile, Patrice responded, "Mother, since God has blessed us so much this year, instead of buying each other gifts, why don't we just buy some of my favorite patients gifts? And, instead of having a big Christmas dinner, what would you think about us working in the homeless shelter helping prepare and serve dinner to the less fortunate?" I said, "That sounds great, Punky."

All I could do was weep for joy, for I knew that the Lord had totally delivered my daughter from depression and restored her joy. She was once again my precious, bubbly and happy Patrice Reneê.

Another miracle. What an awesome God!

13

Patrice Departs to Her Heavenly Home

It was early Tuesday morning following the weekend of our Christmas in October and Patrice did not have to go to school or work that day, so I just let her sleep in. The day seemed as normal as any other day when I went downstairs to make coffee, drink my customary three cups, and intercede for my family, fellow Christians and ministers. After worshiping God, I went upstairs to get dressed and when I was ready for work, I went to Patrice's room, knelt at her bedside, and hugged and kissed her as I always did. I would tell her, "Patrice, next to the Lord Jesus, I love you more than anything or anyone." Since Patrice had been through so much in her life, I made sure every day before I left that I reassured her of my love. She always responded with the same affirmation back to me, but this time there was no response, yet her stunning crystal blue eyes were open. Like looking into a beautiful, clear ocean. I stared into her eyes and called her name repeatedly, but she did not respond. I began patting her face and continued to call her name, and a crushing blow, I realized that my precious angel was not responding because she was not breathing.

In a state of shock, I immediately called 911, and I can only remember saying, "My baby's not breathing, my baby is not breathing!" The rest was a blur. The dispatcher stayed on the phone with me until the Kannapolis police department and paramedics came immediately. I can only suppose that my phone number must have given her my address because I did not recall giving her any information other than the words of a mother in shock. The paramedics stayed upstairs with Patrice, and I believe it was Lieutenant May who took me downstairs. Before I knew it, my house was filled with people. I just remember sitting in the middle of the living room telling everyone there what a miracle Patrice was.

Transporting Patrice into the ambulance, the detective notified me that she had passed away and that they would have to take her to the hospital to make it official. Weeping uncontrollably, I groaned from the very depths of my being as I continued to go deeper into a state of shock as my heart was severely crushed. I am not sure who called my pastor or friends, but as the detective was leaving, my house filled up with friends and loved ones to support and mourn with me. My family was notified in West Virginia of the tragic news so that they would come and bring their condolences.

While I was still dazed, the Lord brought to my remembrance a vision Patrice had had years before that gave me an unsettling feeling every time she told me. She had visions and visitations of Jesus and she longed to be with Him. He showed her various things that would take place on earth; one that has already happened since her departure is the tragedy of September 11, 2001. Her desire was for the Lord to take her home before these events started to take place. I would say, "Please don't say that, Patrice. You know how much Mother loves you, and I couldn't imagine life without you." She would respond, "I mean it Mother. I have asked the Lord to take me home," and those words stayed close to my heart. Her aspirations were on heavenly things and less on earthly matters. Because of her great love for Jesus, she lived a life of devotion, almost angelic in her attitude as she stood apart from many people. I suppose you could say that once someone experiences the touch and visitation of Jesus, what could be greater than that, it would be the ultimate desire to be with Him. God had sent her here as a special gift for me, and I personally have never known anyone as dedicated and pure in heart as Patrice was. I loved her so dearly and did not want to let her go, but God answered her prayer and took her home.

The grief and pain was indescribable as the days progressed and the reality of what had happened began to settle in. At times, all I could do was weep and cry out to God, feeling like my whole inside had been ripped out. When friends came to pay a visit, they would question why my Christmas tree was up so early, and then as I would convey the events that took place, I recognized the divine inspiration involved in our early Christmas. Jesus knew that Patrice would be celebrating our Lord's birth with the angels in Heaven, but Jesus loved me enough to let me have one more Christmas with my precious daughter. Even though it seemed that Christmas in October was out of season, it was very much in season for Patrice and me.

Unexpectedly, a few weeks prior Patrice had asked me, "Mother, if I died, do you think that my dad would come to my funeral? He never came to see me any other time, not even when I sang for the Charlotte Hornets and offered him free tickets. He didn't even come to my graduation, Mother. Do you think he would come to my funeral?" I responded to Patrice, "I can't answer that question; only God knows." From the time Patrice was a little girl she always wanted her true father's love and acceptance. She cried many tears as she would try to call him, but he seldom returned any of her phone calls. Now I had to call Patrice's dad, but this time I barely could get the words out that Patrice had passed away. He had a few questions and then I told him I needed help. With no insurance on her or money in the bank, I would have to take care of arrangements. In view of that I needed to know if he would be willing to share the expenses of the funeral. I anticipated his response, but it still did not make things any better when he re-plied that he absolutely would not help with the bill. I may have felt better if I believed that he could not afford it, but I had my reservations and my gift of faith was challenged once again.

As my friend Celeste picked me up and drove me to the funeral home to set up arrangements for the service, she began to advise me, "Patricia, honey, you don't have any money or insurance and she is not my daughter, she's yours." I felt she was letting me know that it was my responsibility and not hers, but anyone who knows me very well, understands that I am very responsible and would never want to make anyone accountable for me. Even though she was telling the truth, most people in my position would have been shaken up, but I wasn't, for I knew that the God I serve is faithful. Psalm 37:25 states, *"I have been young, and now am old; yet have I not seen the righteous forsaken, nor his seed begging bread"*.

The peace of God that "passes all understanding" came upon me as if the heavenly hosts surrounded me, and all I could feel was the glory of God. I could not give place to doubt and unbelief, for it is not the nature of faith according to Hebrews 11:1, which states, *"Faith is the substance of things hoped for, the evidence of things not seen"*. Celeste, acting more as a Godmother than a friend, decided to speak on my behalf and introduced herself to the funeral director. She then told him the story concerning Patrice's situation and that I had no money or insur-ance, to which the funeral director responded by advising me to use moderation in making arrangements and keep expenses down. With good intentions, he did not want to see me struggle with paying the funeral costs over a lifetime nor did he want to have an unresolved bill. I began to weep and said, "That girl was my life." In the midst of my pain, God's presence continued to strengthen me with His peace, and all I wanted was the best of everything for Patrice.

The funeral director accompanied Celeste and me to look at the available cas-kets and went over miscellaneous details concerning the service and burial ar-rangements. Both he and Celeste recommended a moderately priced casket, which would be the one he personally would choose as well, but my heart was moved in another way. All I could think of was that Jesus was King of kings and was the only husband and Father Patrice and I had. I could not imagine the King letting His daughter depart to her heavenly home in anything less than the very best. It was at that time that I stated to the funeral director, "I want only the best of everything for my daughter, for her Father is the King." I carefully selected and planned for the funeral service, choosing only the very best money could buy, for I knew the Lord would help me; He has never failed me nor will He ever.

Mr. Whitley, the funeral director, led us back to his office to itemize all the things I had selected, and before he finished, he suggested that I should substitute some of my choices for something a little less expensive. "No, sir," I said, "I told you exactly what I wanted and I want only the best for my daughter." Shocked, he and Celeste both looked on in amazement. He said, "Do you realize you have to pay one-third of the total amount today? I said, "No, sir, but that won't be a problem." I proceeded to take my checkbook out and confidently wrote a check for $3,500 as they watched in disbelief. Although I only had forty dollars in the bank at the time, it was an occasion when I needed to make a withdrawal from my heavenly bank account. Haggai 2:8 states, *"The silver is mine, and the gold is mine saith the* Lord *of the Hosts."* Even though I did not have the money, I knew God did.

He proceeded to ask me if I knew that the remainder must be paid within ninety days. I said, "No, sir, but that won't be a problem," and they remained bewildered by my calm behavior. When he totaled the invoice, he handed it to me, so I took the bill, stood to my feet, and held it up toward Heaven. I wanted witnesses to verify God's miracle-working power, so I asked both Celeste and the funeral director, "Would you please watch me?" I began to pray aloud, "Now, Father God, in the name of Jesus, the Word says that the mother is to bear children and the man is to labor. I have always paid my tithes and given offerings, and I have raised my child to the best of my knowledge. I have been faithful on my part and now this bill is not mine, it's Yours, for you are the only Father Patrice has and the only husband that I have." It was at that point that I knew I had touched the throne room of God, and it was as if Jesus was standing right there beside me. I had perfect peace knowing that my God, the God of Abraham, Isaac, Jacob, and Patricia, would provide for Patrice and me.

We then went to the florist and I selected an elegant shade of lavender for the roses that would adorn the top of her casket and requested to purchase all that they had in that shade. Having more than one hundred roses in supply, the florist asked how many I wanted. "All of them," I replied, and the flowers arrayed on the casket and in the funeral home were absolutely magnificent.

I was surprised to come home and find my brother Paul and niece Kathy already there from West Virginia. Kathy and I were upstairs when the phone rang and. Paul, Jr., stood at the bottom of the stairs and said, "Trish, you need to take this call; this sounds important." My dear friend on the phone started talking, "Trish, you have been through enough. You don't need any more stress. My husband and I have prayed and agreed, and the Lord had put in our hearts to pay for Patrice's funeral in full." My heart was so overwhelmed to know that someone loved Patrice and me enough to provide for her departure. I began to cry and said, "You don't understand. I chose the best of everything. It was the most expensive funeral that money could buy. You don't understand how much it is." She said, "I know exactly how much it is." I then informed her that I wrote a check for $3,500 in faith believing that God would make a way, but I did not have enough money in the bank to cover the check. She reassured me that she would call the funeral director and inform him that payment would be made in full first thing the following morning, and to hold my check and give it back to her when the invoice was satisfied.

The next day at the funeral home, the funeral director looked at me and said, "Mrs. Thomas, the funeral bill has been paid in full," and I said, "Didn't I tell you that it would be?" In humility he said, "Mrs. Thomas, I never met anyone like you before." To which I replied, "Don't worry about it; you never will again." In 1 Peter 2:9, the Word states, *"But ye are a chosen generation, a royal priesthood, an holy nation, a peculiar people; that ye should shew forth the praises of him who has called you out of darkness into his marvelous light"*. Sometimes we may seem different to other people, but His ways are higher than ours, and the walk of faith will take us to where angels fear to tread.

At that moment, I could once again testify that I have never known God to fail. We have to hold fast to our faith and not waver. My princess would be buried with the royal burial she deserved, and the King of kings, my husband and her Father, took care of everything.

Another miracle. What an awesome God!

14

Patrice's Funeral

In tribute to Patrice, the preordained time came to bury my precious daughter as well as honor and eulogize her life and many achievements. With the room filled with flowers, friends, family, fellow Christians and ministers, people came through the line to pay their respects. The whole situation seemed so surreal. I remember standing there with my niece Kathy, wondering how all these people knew what had happened so quickly. The line seemed to be never ending, and some individuals came from hundreds of miles away to pay their respects and offer comfort.

Kathy and I had put together a display on the table beside her casket to showcase all of Patrice's accomplishments. It included various pictures, the sash from the beauty contest, her saxophone, and most treasured trophy; the Christian Character Award presented to her at her high school graduation. Even in that desperate hour, I wanted her testimony to be heard. The fragrance from the flowers delicately permeated the room, and an indescribable peace settled in the midst of the many emotions of shock, grief, disbelief, heartache and unrelenting sorrow.

Fifteen minutes before the funeral was to begin, Patrice's father walked into the funeral home. I will never forget the look on his face when he saw the table displaying all of Patrice's deeds along with the picture of her and Peter. He carefully reviewed the portions of her life in amazement and said he was not aware of her winning a beauty pageant, to which I replied, "You would have known if you would have returned her call two weeks ago." As he kept looking over all the things he had missed, with great remorse he said repeatedly that he did not know about these things. I repeated, "You would have known, if you would only have returned her calls." He was crying uncontrollably when he approached the casket.

My heart was full of compassion for him. As I continued to watch him struggle with guilt, I went into deep thought about our lives together and our difficult marriage. I no longer had regret because out of that union came our beautiful daughter Patrice. I told him, "The Holy Ghost is the greatest gift I have ever had, but next to Jesus, Patrice was my second greatest gift. You had a part in bringing Patrice into my life and because of that, I will always love you." It was not that I was "in love" with him, but I had a choice to make. I could choose to remind him of how he neglected her and broke her little heart so many times or make the godly choice of walking in unconditional love, as Christ loves us.

As Christians, we all have times when we are faced with temptations to give in to our hurts, which are times of testing. It is in times like this that we have the privilege to make the right choice where our love for God is greater than our own disappointments. I chose to be a more excellent and mature Christian that day; not bitter, but better, even in the midst of my deepest pain. It was a time to dispense forgiveness as he kept hugging me and weeping. He said, "You were the best mother in the world." I could not have received a higher compliment, and valued that moment of closure for Patrice, who had suffered so from the neglect of her father.

Mark 11:25-26 tells of the importance and the necessity of forgiveness. Many people cannot understand how I forgave him so easily that day, or how I walk in forgiveness for the many things I encounter daily. As the Father forgives us, it is imperative that we forgive others quickly. If we do not forgive, neither will our heavenly Father forgive our trespasses. The Bible says we all fall short of the glory of God. We are all at the mercy of our Father's forgiveness. I have always believed that a person needs to be quick to believe, quick to repent, and quick to forgive. Remember the lady in the Bible who was going to be stoned? Where was the Christian love that would cover the multitude of her sins? All her accusers had stones to throw, yet they all had sin. However, Jesus spoke right to the core issue and no one could cast the first stone. When they really examined themselves, they realized that they too were unworthy. Unforgiveness opens many doors of bitterness and anger. Forgiveness gives us the grace to walk in love, bringing peace and the blessing of God. I knew that God would bless me if I extended mercy, because I would then obtain mercy as well. Lost in thought of God's forgiveness, I was startled back into the reality of the occasion.

The moment had come for the closing of the casket and I just stood there unable to move; it seemed as though time stood still. I was captivated by the peaceful expression on my daughter's face and leaned in to hold onto her. I began to groan in deep despair, not wanting to let go and give my daughter up, but my niece put her hand on my back and said, "Trisha, it's time." With my heart sink-ing and my strength drained, she helped me stand up as we watched the funeral director close the casket. The reality of knowing that I would never see her again on this earth consumed my thoughts. All I can remember was following the casket into the chapel. My feet were moving, but I was numb. When we entered the chapel, that is when I began to experience to an even greater magnitude the finality and impact of the situation. There were people I had not seen in years and some I did not even know. Two of the most respected preachers in Kannapolis, North Carolina, were presiding over the service: Pastor Gary Sheets from Metro Worship Center and Rev. Sam Crisp from West A Church of God. Some of the finest musicians in the area came together and chose the perfect music for the service: Steve Allman playing the piano, Toni Bogart-Syvrud and Betsy Covington Graham singing, along with Peter Nemeth playing saxophone. It was very moving, and I had no idea how that beautiful service came together.

As the ministers began to share, their words of comfort strengthened me and those who knew and loved Patrice. I will never forget Pastor Gary telling the congregation that God knew Patrice would be called into Heaven, but Patrice and I were blessed with the opportunity to share a final Christmas together. Even though it was out of season, it was very much in season for Patrice and me. Pastor Crisp spoke about the amazing bond Patrice and I shared and of her devout love for God. So kind were his words when he stated that no one else could have been the mother to Patrice that I had been. That was one of the most meaningful things anyone could ever say about Patrice and myself.

The atmosphere set by the musicians brought a heart-warming glow of reassurance from the first solo Peter played on his saxophone in honor of his true love, "My Endless Love," to the pure worship that came as Toni sang "I Could Sing of Your Love Forever." The Spirit of the Lord fell upon me, and as I stood to my feet, I lifted my hands and began to worship the Lord even in the darkest hour of my life. Like King David said in Psalm 34:1, *"I will bless the Lord at all times: his praise shall continually be in my mouth"*. I could feel the presence of God and the whole congregation joined me in reverencing the Lord. The glory was so strong that as I held my hands up to Jesus, I was enveloped in peace: it was the most glorious funeral I have ever witnessed. Even though it was a funeral with tears and weeping, still the presence of God kept us under a covering of peace. I know that a lot of people have wondered how I kept my sanity through all of this, but the Word of God declares, *"Thou wilt keep him in perfect peace, whose mind is stayed on thee: because he trusteth in thee"*, ... *"being confident of this very thing, that he which hath begun a good work in you will perform it until the day of Jesus Christ"* (Isaiah 26:3; Philippians 1:6).

Patrice had a funeral that was fitting for a princess; after all, she was the daughter of a king, the King of all kings, and I could not imagine anything less. The Lord has been faithful to provide for Patrice and me in every aspect of our lives. I could never have orchestrated such a glorious and beautiful funeral, but God did it for me. Words can never express the depth of my heartfelt loss and how much I miss my precious daughter, Patrice. I am consoled knowing that she is truly in a better place with her Master of Love. She will never have to face rejection, sickness, persecution, or any other heartache again because to be absent from the body is to be present with Him. I know that one day I will be with her and my precious Lord Jesus Christ.

Another miracle. What an awesome God!

SECTION VII

A Tribute to Patrice

Dad and me at the Church Dinner

Me, Patricia Thomas

"For the promise is to you and your children..."
Patrice's father

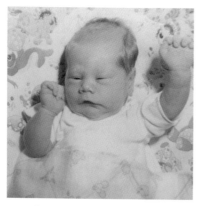

Birth Picture, Patrice Harrold

Patrice, 4 years old

Patrice, 6 years old

Dreams really do come true

Patrice at 17

Senior Graduation

Peter meets the girl of his dreams.

Such an annointed saxaphone player >>

Your son and daughters shall prophesy...

Rev. Jerry Dudson
"and I will set up shephers over them which shall feed them..." Uncle Jerry

Prophet H. Richard Hall with Patrice

*Margaret Faye and
James Black*

*Our dear friend
Brother H.B. Love*

"I am the God that healeth thee..."

Patrice and Patricia ministering together

I love the children

The blue house

always time for shopping

*ministering at
Mother's Day
Conference*

Patricia with Pastors Pauline Knight and May Walker in Jamaica

Pastor's wife, Rosa Zapata and teachers

Patricia praying in the streets

Patricia at Wailing Wall Jerusalem

Mission Impossible, 22 boxes to Jamaica

Toni Bogard-Syvrud, my dear friend and book co-laborer

Kathy Kress, my niece, helping with my book

Give thanks to the LORD, for he is good... Psalm 136:1

*Taste and see that the LORD is good; blessed is the man
who takes refuge in him. Psalm 34:8*

Forever Friends
by Jade Woodall

My friend, you left behind a void
That weighs so heavy on my heart.
Our lives once joined together
Have now suddenly been torn apart.

You were like my sister
More than you were my friend.
My heart aches for this loss
And I fear it may never mend.

I wish I could have told you good-bye
Before the Lord took you away.
Please know I cherish you, friend,
And I will celebrate you every day.

The Lord was very kind to bless me
With a friendship that was rare.
But your absence in my life now
Is almost too much for me to bear.

I pray the Lord will give me grace
Throughout this trying time.
And for all the friends He could have given me
I am so glad that He made you mine.

I will miss you always and forever, Patrice,
But I know now that you have peace.
You are in sweet, beautiful Paradise
Where all your pain has been released.

In Memory of Patrice Harrold

1

Patrice's Prophecy Is Fulfilled
(September 11, 2001)

"Mother, don't go to bed just yet, the Lord is showing me a vision…"

In reflecting over the many experiences we had together, the joys, the sorrows, the love we shared, and the depth of friendship I had with my daughter, I began to understand the beauty and purpose of this rare rose. Just as a rose captured in the peak of its beauty, its unforgettable fragrance stays with us beyond its delicate life. Her way of life, her deeds and the words, she said exemplified devotion and dedication to God in such a noble measure that she became my inspiration. God loved me so much, that He let me have Patrice here on earth for twenty two and a half years, but her heavenly scent lingered on, for she was my angel sent from Heaven to make my life more complete as a mother. God had bestowed many talents upon her to sing, prophesy and play instruments, which she used throughout her life to glorify God as long as she was on planet earth. She diligently studied the Word and applied herself to seek the face of God and the word of the Lord grew mighty in her. One of the more profound and relevant words was given to her when she was very young, and I believe that this shed light on some of my heartfelt questions about her youthful life coming to such an early end.

It was late one night after watching the news when suddenly Patrice said, "Mother! I see New York City on fire! Her little eyes opened wide as she saw in panoramic view buildings going up in flames and people screaming and running in terror. In the fear of the Lord, I considered how the Spirit of God was moving upon my daughter, and chills came to me as she continued. "I see foreign nations coming against the American financial system. It is all so sad, for I see many hurting people. There are drug addicts, Satan worshipers and demon-possessed people on the streets." I could see the burden of the Lord weigh on her precious heart, and I knew she could not have contrived this in her own mind. She had prophetic insight that was far beyond her years. She began to tell me, "Mother, we do not need to build any more buildings. The church needs to go to the streets and minister deliverance to these people."

My heart was troubled when she kept on, "Mother, when these things start taking place or happening, I have asked the Lord Jesus to take me home. This will be the beginning of the tragic things that will be happening in the last days and I don't want to be here." Imploring her not to say such unsettling things, I responded, "Please don't say that Patrice, because the Bible says you can have whatever you say." Patrice, being the Bible scholar that she was, already knew what the Word of God said, but she insisted, "I mean it, Mother. I want Jesus to take me home."

With her prayer answered, the Lord took Patrice Harrold home for eternity on October 25, 2000. This prophecy was given when Patrice was approximately eleven years old, and was fulfilled September 11, 2001, a year following her departure to her heavenly home. The Word of God plainly states, in Amos 3:7, *"Surely the LORD GOD will do nothing, but he revealeth his secret unto his servants the prophets."*

Section VIII

*Birds of a Feather Flock
Together But Eagles Fly Alone*

1

Eagles Fly Alone

I never imagined my life taking the turn it did, and now I was alone soaring like an eagle with an empty nest. It is amazing to see how walking with God through life's experiences can create fortitude of character, giving strength you never thought possible. When my husband Gerald left, it was very difficult as well as heartrending. Although my faith was strong, my dreams of raising my daughter with a father and having a family unit that served God came to a sudden end, and so I felt alone and overwhelmed. When I came to terms with it and recognized that Jesus was the only father for Patrice and my true husband, I started to heal. Regardless of who left or whatever difficult circumstances I faced, I was determined to raise my daughter in a godly, committed fashion, and I knew He would provide; He would be my cloud by day and fire by night. He would be the father, and I would be the mother; for some trust in chariots and horses, but my trust was in God. After Patrice left, there were no words that could express the magnitude of pain. There were times that I would cry enough tears to fill a rive,r for next to the Lord, I loved that child more than anything or anyone.

I could not understand why I was left alone to carry on the ministry, when it was both Gerald and Patrice who were the talented ones with the potential to be mighty ministers for God; here I was with nothing to offer except my love. Ultimately, I knew that Patrice was in a better place, but that did not make me miss her any less. Her companionship and friendship had so often given me the courage and purpose to keep moving forward. Now my trust in God and understanding that He knew what was best for me became the guiding force to help me navigate through the downpour of heartfelt thoughts. My heart clung to the truth that He would never leave me nor forsake me, even in the darkest night. His love was special for me, for I had the awesome opportunity to serve and minister to my family and His precious people. I had no alternative but to move forward with my life and walk in the destiny set before me with renewed determination, alone with God. There is a time when we have to face God and eternity alone. Many people are afraid of being alone, but that became my meditation and strength; so I began to create the atmosphere to evoke His presence. I began to understand that my Maker was my husband, and my heart of worship burst into revival flames consecrating to an even greater measure my love for Him. As Romans 8:38-39 reaffirmed my heartfelt faith, I was persuaded, *"that neither death, nor life, nor angels, nor principalities, nor powers, nor things present, nor things to come, nor height, nor depth, nor any other creature"* could ever separate me from the love of God which is in Christ Jesus.

As my devotion grew, my vision developed with clarity to see how I would have grace to walk in signs, miracles and wonders. My heart was to win millions of souls to the Kingdom of God and minister healing to crippled, blind and hurting people. I have always had great love and compassion for God's people, especially orphans and handicapped children. I believe that God allows us to walk through things so that we have authority over things. It is because of those places of deep hurt I had walked in, that I would now have authority to help others find comfort and healing for their abandoned lives. Though I was not physically blind, there were times in my life when I had to *"lift up mine eyes to the hills, from whence cometh my help"* and see with eyes of faith instead of looking at the storms facing me. There were so many places I had to walk where even angels feared to tread, but I was able to confront my fears. My faith soared high like an eagle, and only the eagle has the ability to lock its wings and soar above the storm. The purpose of the storms in our lives is to allow the eagle to ascend higher, and actually escape the tempest; so it is with our journey of spiritual flight. As wine is made from grapes that are crushed, and perfume is extracted from flowers that are pressed beyond measure, so my ministry was birthed out of my pain.

In order to have a relationship with anyone, you must be willing to spend time with them. If you really have a good friend, you will want to spend time with them doing everything. You will want to dine with them, and you will want to share your accomplishments and disappointments, your blessings, your failures and your life. That is the same way God wants us to be with Him. He is always there to listen, understand and comfort you, and He always has the answer to all your concerns in His Holy Word. I value my relationship with Him because of His great sacrifice of love for me. I now know what it is to enter into and partake of the suffering of Christ. However, I also recognize what it is for Jesus to identify with my sufferings. I am redeemed from sin, sickness and poverty, and someday I will be able to make heaven my home. There is absolutely no other friend I have revered more than Jesus. He is Jehovah Jireh, my provider, Jehovah Rapha, my healer, and Jehovah Nissi, my banner of love.

There are two foremost guiding principles that I follow, which have kept me consistent through my journey. First, I never question God; I just trust Him, for I know He knows me better than I know myself. Secondly, I get up in the morning with the "attitude of gratitude," worshiping the Lord and thanking Him for giving me another day of life, no matter what the circumstances. My most intimate and treasured times of worship come when I am home alone with Jesus. I do not answer my door or phone at this time, for nothing can ever take the place of the peace I feel when I am in the presence of the Lord. With a spirit of thanksgiving, I sing and dance before Him and ask Him to use me to glorify Him during the day. He paid the ultimate price and died on the cross for someone as imperfect as myself. I am overwhelmed with His great love and often find myself sitting for hours weeping before Him. There are times when an extraordinary sense of God's presence comes over me. It feels like a blanket of love, which covers my entire being, stays on me for a while, and then suddenly lifts. Many other supernatural manifestations confirm that the presence of God is with me. Our divine romance is new every morning, as if one was on a honeymoon. After I have thanked God for all His goodness and mercy, only then do I even begin to make intercession for my family, friends, ministers and fellow Christians. Faith and provision come after we first minister to Him, because if we take care of His needs first, then He will lavishly pour out of His abundance on us.

2

Intimacy With Jesus

"For many are called, but few are chosen" (Matthew 22:14). In the Song of Solomon the bride and the daughters of Jerusalem are interested in the bridegroom. Both are *"called,"* but only the bride is *"chosen,"* as there is a noticeable difference in their comments about the one to whom they relate.

The bride is seen as being intensely in love, and she gives an intimate description of the one she loves. She has a single eye, and seeks only the bridegroom.

His mouth is most sweet: yea, he is altogether lovely. This is my beloved, and this is my friend, O daughters of Jerusalem (Song of Solomon 5:16).

The daughters of Jerusalem had been given the same opportunity to respond.

I charge you, O daughters of Jerusalem, if ye find my beloved, that you tell Him, that I am sick of love (Song of Solomon 5:8).

There is a difference between being in love, and just loving someone. The bride prefers a honeymoon relationship, as she longs to be with the bridegroom. However, when questioned, the daughters said,

What is thy beloved more than another beloved, that thou dost so charge us? (Song of Solomon 5:9)

They prefer a casual friendship, and consider the bridegroom to be merely "another beloved." These daughters are seeking many things and, therefore, they have no desire to be with him. They do not have a "single eye": *"What is he more than another?"*

The bride, therefore, was chosen, because she seeks an intimate relationship with her love, and desires to be alone with him: *"Tell him, that I am sick of [deeply in] love."*

> *Who is this that cometh up from the wilderness, leaning upon her beloved?*
> (Song of Solomon 8:5).

For us to have an intimate relationship with Jesus, we must be willing to spend much time alone with Him, and find satisfaction in being in His presence. The "daughters of Jerusalem" are satisfied with a religious service "about" the Lord, and with all the "things" that He can provide for them, rather than seeking an intimate relationship with the Lord.

Unfortunately, today, all too many "Christians" can be compared to the daughters of Jerusalem, rather than to the bride.

For those of us who truly seek the Lord Himself, it is satisfying to know that when we rest in His presence, and commune with Him, we are among the chosen.

Written by Patricia Thomas
Published in *The Bannerr*, Winter 2003

Part 2

A Life after Patrice

SECTION I

*Who Will
Go For Me?*

The Great Commission
Matthew 16:15

Mission Impossible

Go to Jerusalem, Judea and the uttermost part of the earth. Acts 1:8
A strong woman has faith and strength for the journey.
A woman of faith knows that it is in the journey that she will become strong.

Through the years, I knew that I would serve God and go to the nations, but I never knew, the price would be so high. Where did He want me to go? What was I to do? I was reminded of the prophecies I had received from Brother Hall and many other ministers in the past, that someday I would become a mother to children on foreign soil. When Patrice and I were ministering in Jerusalem several years ago, a prophetic word was given by one of the ministers in the church. She said Jerusalem was only the launching pad for me, for the Lord would send me from nation to nation, and that at times, I would even minister to some people who were royalty. However, it would all happen so quickly that I wouldn't have time to say, "But Lord, what about my daughter?" Patrice said, "Mother, that frightened me when she said you would go from nation to nation. I don't want you leaving me." I remembered reassuring Patrice that I would not go until she was taken care of. By that I meant, finished college and happily married, but the Lord had something else in mind. I began to pray and ask God if He really wanted me to be a missionary.

Reflecting back on the reasons for my passion to tell everyone about Jesus, I was reminded of Patrice's prophecy concerning September 11, and the vision of

New York City in flames. I remember how my heart felt as she conveyed the destitute condition of the many unsaved people in her vision. They were in the streets; some were on drugs, while others were bound by alcohol, all demonized in some way or another. They had one thing in common; all of them needed someone to come and minister hope to them. We the church must go to the streets and minister deliverance to these people. God so loved the world that He gave His only Son. When everything that was close to me was taken away, I had to draw near to God and step forward to the next level.

Also, in my life's journey I realized that I was not perfect, just forgiven. To go from glory to glory and reach the next level, I had to be refined and purified as gold. Job said, *"But he knoweth the way that I take: when he hath tried me, I shall come forth as gold"* (Job 23:10). The heat was being turned up a little, but the Master Refiner was calling me to a place of greater consecration and preparing me for the nations. When a master refiner purifies gold or silver, he places the gold in a furnace. He leaves it in for a while and then pulls it out to check it for impurities and dross. If he sees that there are still impurities and dross which surface, he scrapes off the top of the gold and places it back in the furnace. He then turns the heat up even more, enabling a more intense purification process. The gold is ready for use when the master refiner sees a reflection of his face in the gold, like one who looks into a mirror. That is the way our Master, Jesus, is with us. When He sees His reflection in us, then and only then are we really ready for His use. More than anything, I wanted the Lord to see His reflection in me.

During this time of seeking God's will, I would experience renewal of strength and direction like Isaiah, who saw the Lord high and lifted up. Isaiah reckoned with himself and saw his humanity. Was the Master's reflection in his life? What did God see when he looked into this great prophet? Isaiah became great because he was honest about what he saw, a man of unclean lips. It is time to stop hiding behind our walls of indifference, fear and pride. In the light of this encounter with God, Isaiah would be changed forever. He cried out to God, *"I am undone."* It wasn't until he allowed the Lord to purge his heart, and touch his lips with the coal from the altar, that he could hear the voice of the Lord speak, *"Whom shall I send, and who will go for us? Then said I, Here am I; send me"* (Isaiah 6:8).

I was undone, but now my heart yielded to the voice of the Lord, and I too could say, "Lord, send me" God broke into my life, so that He could break out of my life. This would be the experience that would give me the heart for the Great Commission. If we want to hear from God, we must look for that open door of heaven. John the Revelator turned to see a door open in Heaven, even though he was a prisoner on the isle of Patmos. It wasn't about what his present condition was, but to hear the proceeding word of God call him to, *"Come up hither, and I will show thee things which must be hereafter"*(Revelation 4:1). We must be willing to stand in His presence and hear the voice of the Lord commission us, because the only way of going through is by going up. We are waiting on God, but in this day and age, God is waiting on us.

I was to learn that going into the mission field would be an unexpected source of invaluable lessons in my journey through life. The call commissioned me to go therefore and teach in all nations, baptizing them in the name of the Lord, witnessing to the brokenhearted. I would go from nation to nation preaching the Gospel of Jesus Christ. I became more determined to win a million souls to the Kingdom of God while here on the great planet earth.

If it was important for Jesus to come to earth in person for a lost and dying world, then we must do the same, for the servant is not greater than the master. We are His hands and His feet, and the harvest is ripe, but the workers are few. *"Whom shall I send?"* Will you go?

2

If It's God's Will, It's God's Bill

After fasting for seven days, I awoke to a beautiful spring day. As I was meditating and beholding God's wondrous creation, I received a phone call that came as an answer to my prayers the night before. God's timing is so precise. I'm thankful for faith-filled Christians who are obedient to God's voice. Even when they don't necessarily understand the outcome, it activates faith. On this occasion, it was a friend of mine named Laura who told me she had a dream about a missionary. At first she thought the missionary in her dream was a friend of hers who has been a missionary to many different countries, to whom she affectionately refers as the "Missionary Lady." To her surprise, when the "Missionary Lady" in her dream turned around, she realized it wasn't her friend, but I was the "Missionary Lady." What confused her more was that I was dressed like her friend wearing the same identical outfit. Sensing that this dream was significant and from God, she felt impressed to call me. Although she didn't understand her dream, I did, for it confirmed God's directions and I thanked Him for affirmation.

Now the question remained about the specific place I would be sent to. Within a few hours of Laura's call, Jimmy White, a missionary and prophet, called. Often- times, the telephone has been a great source of communication between the throne room and me. Jimmy told me he felt led of the Spirit to return to Jamaica for a short-term missions trip and asked if I would consider making a donation to support the cost of the trip. One might think of Jamaica as the beautiful place shown on travel brochures; however, within minutes of the cities, there is vast poverty and neglected children who are in desperate need. Since he was asking for contributions from people he knew, he asked me to call some of my friends as well. Later that evening, he called to see if anyone had responded. I told him that I had contacted several people, but they had already made pledges to other ministries. I continued to tell him that I was praying and asking the Lord specifically how I could help. Although I didn't have any extra money, I had a credit card and would be willing to charge his airfare. I know it's not God's will for His people to be in debt, but I was expecting God to help me since it was a gift to spread the Gospel. Jimmy said he would pay me back, but I refuted, "Absolutely not! According to the Bible, if I give to a prophet, I will receive a prophet's reward." Immediately after I was off the phone, I called and ordered the ticket.

Moments later, the phone rang again. Reverend Thelma Wilkins was calling me concerning the trip. Although she was not impressed to help Jimmy at that time, she truly believed that I was supposed to go to Jamaica, and that God would have supernatural connections for me once I got there. There was my answer, as to where to go, but now that I had charged Jimmy's ticket, I told her that I really didn't have the money. When she was curious as to why I would charge his ticket, I continued to explain how I knew that he was such a blessing to the people in the area of Chester Castle, and that we should support him not only as a friend but as a prophet as well. Amazingly, after I talked with her, Jimmy called again and said, "Patricia, I really feel impressed in my spirit that you should go and help me minister to the needs of the people. They will love you!" After these two conversations, I believe that the Holy Spirit was directing my footsteps, and that it was God's will for me to go to Jamaica. So, I got off the phone and charged a ticket for myself. I often say, "If it is God's will, then it is His bill; if it is my will, then it is my bill."

The phone was ringing again, and it was my friend Thelma calling back to reiterate the strong witness in her spirit that God had connections for me in Jamaica. I told her, "Well, guess what? I have already charged a ticket." I explained how Prophet White had called back and asked me to help him minister. She asked about my cost involved and sent a check to cover my airfare because she knew I had been called of the Lord to go to Jamaica and would have supernatural connections.

Do you see how God works? I blessed the prophet, believing that God would reward me. While I was on my way to work a few days later, I was thanking God for His provision for my trip to Jamaica, but I was still indebted for the prophet's airfare. I knew that Jimmy was a blessing to the people of Jamaica, so I asked for the Lord to please help me pay the bill, not telling anyone else but just God. That same day, while I was working, a young lady who was a coworker came up to me and told me that she needed to discuss something important with me. It seemed that she had been concerned because she had not been paying her tithes. However, this particular year she was going to receive a tax refund and felt led to tithe the tax refund to my ministry, which covered the complete cost of the ticket I had purchased for Jimmy.

Another miracle. What an awesome God!

3

The Bush Country of Chester Castle

As part of the preparation for this mission trip, our team packed twenty-eight suitcases full of beans, rice, medical supplies, candy and other items that were considered luxuries by the people of the bush country, things that we take for granted every day. The day had come to check in at the airport with our assortment of mismatched suitcases, and it was quite a sight to behold. We were so excited, and with great anticipation, looked forward to arriving at our destination within a few hours. Finally boarding the plane, we took off for Jamaica. To pass the time, we shared ministry stories and experiences that we had had in previous meetings, and it was a glorious time of reflection in the Lord. As the plane soared through the heavens, I could hardly wait to see all of the precious children. Without even the slightest hint of turbulence, our plane finally landed in Montego Bay. After we made our way through customs, the Jamaican people who were there to welcome us loaded the truck and we began our journey to Chester Castle. I'm serious when I say that the driver was going over one hundred miles an hour through the bumpy, winding roads. Trust me, I considered it a miracle to arrive safely, alive and in one piece, exiting the vehicle without injury.

We arrived in the early afternoon at the house where we would be staying during our trip, each of us having our own room. Since it was my first trip to Jamaica, I really did not know what to expect, but I just could hardly wait to see the children. When we arrived at our humble abode, it was a poorly constructed shanty that had been painted an odd shade of turquoise on the outside. The outhouse was about five hundred feet from the house and it was too appalling for words, so we won't go there. Inside, the walls had scenic drawings of trees and flowers; however, someone had marred the walls with graffiti. In my bedroom, sunlight was shining through the boarded windows while the earth was peeking up through the boards on the floor. In the center of my floor was a very large hole in the already badly boarded floor. That troubled me, knowing that snakes, rodents and other creepy crawlers could easily find their way in. When I told my host, he said, "No problem, man we will fix it." His solution to this dilemma was to just lay the suitcase over the hole. Satisfied that he had fixed this small crisis, he gave me a huge smile and was perfectly content with his clever plan.

Acclimating to my new environment was slightly bewildering, but I couldn't really concentrate on my surroundings because people kept coming into the house, to see what was going on. We distributed some supplies and treats to the families coming to the house as well as greeting people in the village and inviting them to church services for the following evening. Early in the evening I began to fade, and decided to curl up on the mattress. All at once, my legs, arms and face began to tingle. This time it wasn't the Holy Spirit or goose bumps; it was bugs! There they were, hundreds of little bugs, crawling all over the mattress. In response to my shrieking, the man of the house came a second time to my aid. When I could finally gain composure enough to talk to him, I tried to explain my trouble as well as possible. Again, he smiled with satisfaction, for he had thought of another solution to my trivial crisis. His answer to the infestation of the mattress was to put clean sheets on the bed.

Apparently this man had an "out of sight, out of mind" mentality. There is an old adage which says, "If you can't beat them, join them," so with this mindset I attempted to go to sleep. However, my room suddenly began to fill with children who wanted to stay there and just watch me. To my surprise, being uncomfortable was no longer a focus and I did not care about the bugs, floor or anything else that would normally frighten me. There is just something about children and me; they know that I love them and they love me also. Their little eyes cried without tears for some type of hope that they could hold on to. I talked with them, gave treats, hugged and loved them and played until the late hours of the evening. I love Jesus and all of His children, no matter what race, creed, or color.

The next morning, I went out to take a shower in a makeshift bathhouse of sorts. The small structure, crafted from aluminum, was a stall with a pan of water in it, and a door that latched with a coat hanger. After my morning routine, we started out for the church, which was approximately two miles away on foot. With each sunrise, the children joined us, and would help carry our supplies. Their little feet were bare walking on the rocky road, but they didn't seem to mind because they were just so happy to have people there to love them and care for them. I would teach them about Jesus, and they would happily dance with me and sing about the Lord. This was a new idea to them, for they had always been told to be quiet in the church. Out of all the children, however, there was one precious boy named "Did," who was always there and really stood out to me. He was such a sweet child; I just wanted to put him on the plane with us and take him home. Did was nine years old when I first met him, and he would watch me intently, staying by my side every moment of the day. Did would carry our supplies for hours with enthusiasm. He brought so much joy as he would laugh, and he responded with great zeal to dancing before the Lord. It is my desire to this day to give Did a better way of life, because my heart was knitted with his. As a token of appreciation for his kindness, I gave him a special Bible and loaded him down with sweets and tee shirts from America.

After four days, we had exhausted our supplies as we covered many miles going door-to-door, sharing the Gospel, and giving provisions to the residents in the community. From the early morning hours until it was almost dark, we would cover as much ground as possible. On these trips back to the house, you could not see the path before you, and often it was slippery after a rainy day. Nevertheless, we didn't care; we would just sing and praise God all the way back to the house.

I will always remember the little white church at the bottom of the hill where Jimmy and I ministered. The children would come to the services early with the team, and I would share with them how the Lord inhabits the praises of His people. I taught them how to dance before the Lord as the way to express praise in a greater measure, letting them know that it is a delight to come to the house of God. When the music started, immediately the children and I would jump for joy, run, leap and dance with all our might before the Lord just like King David. The smiles on their little faces were radiant, and they were learning that praising the Lord could be fun. The children never seemed to want to go home, and I wasn't sure where they all lived. All I know is that the whole time we were there, they kept coming to our house and staying until the wee hours of the night.

We met a dear woman of God, Sister Solomon, who lived at the bottom of the hill near the church. I told her where we were staying, so she offered for me to stay with her. Her house was different from most of the houses there in the neighborhood, having indoor facilities and a phone. She kept her house immaculate, and even though it would have been a better place to stay, there was not enough room for me, and the other two women who were traveling with us. So I asked for permission to use her phone, and called a nearby Holiday Inn and reserved a room with more suitable accommodations. We all felt that we had done everything we could for the people in that part of Jamaica.

In addition, there was something else I was feeling concerning the house we were staying in. I could not feel any real peace, but it was not because of the holes in the floor or the roaches in the house; it was something about the spirit of the house. Sister Solomon confirmed my insight informing us, that since the passing of their mother (who was the person we were supposed to stay with), the adult children had become involved in drugs and a sinful lifestyle. No wonder I did not feel comfortable there. I did not want to put myself in a dangerous position and I felt that moving to a hotel would be a wise decision, while Jimmy decided he would stay with Sister Solomon a few more days.

4

The Ministry of Tracts

How can they believe if they don't hear?

Leaving Chester Castle now, we would be released to minister and meet other Divine connections anticipated for the trip. Back through the winding roads again I prayed for our safety, but this time we were heading for the hotel. It was hard to believe that within a forty-five-minute drive one could find the beauty that is promised in the brochures for Montego Bay. After we had checked in and situated ourselves in our rooms, I gathered Gospel tracts and started out for a walk on the beach to win souls.

On the beach I stopped to talk to a young woman named Joyce who braided hair for money and to the people who were waiting their turn. As I was sharing the Gospel, a young lady who was visiting from Canada listened intently, visibly getting touched by God's Spirit. When I was finished, she came to me and began to tell me that she had been a Christian all her life, but was now backslidden. To complicate matters, she had become involved in a relationship, she had a daughter born with cerebral palsy, and now the father of the child did not want to marry her or raise the child. Musing over the fact that she had been a Sunday school teacher in a Baptist church, she now felt as though her life was hopeless and that she would no longer be able to come back to God.

I reassured her that God was in the forgiving business and started a verse very familiar to all of us found in 2 Chronicles 7:14, which states, *"If my people, which are called by my name, shall humble themselves, and pray, and seek my face, and turn from their wicked ways; then will I hear from heaven, and will forgive their sin, and will heal their land"*. I went on to explain to her that it was the Lord who was stating that He would forgive "His people" in that verse; it wasn't in reference to "the heathen" finding forgiveness. God knew that "His people" would make mistakes, and that is why He put that verse in the Bible. Jesus wanted to give her a brand new start. I think it is important to know that the Bible declares, in Romans 3:23, *"For all have sinned, and come short of the glory of God"*.

It wasn't until Peter failed that he was able to win five thousand people to the Lord just shortly thereafter. Just because we make mistakes, it is not over. But we must look ahead, just as the apostle Paul stated: in Philippians 3:13-14, *"Brethren, I count not myself to have apprehended: but this one thing I do, forgetting those things which are behind, and reaching forth unto those things which are before. I press toward the mark for the prize of the high calling of God in Christ Jesus"* (KJV). I encouraged her to go back to teaching Sunday school, lay hands on her daughter to pray for her healing, and see what God would do for her.

We must always go back to our first love, for that is where our strength and hope come from. She was really touched when I told her about the dream of my daughter singing before thousands totally healed. Comforted by my testimony of how God healed Patrice, she told me, "If I didn't come to Jamaica for any other reason, then I came here to meet you and hear you today, so that I can have hope for my life, and faith for my daughter's healing." As she spoke, I could feel my heart fill with compassion, and the word of the Lord came to me that we should never give up and always pray without ceasing.

Joyce, intrigued by our conversation, later asked me to come with her after she was finished braiding hair, to the marketplace to meet her sister and friends, who were Christians. Later that day I met up with the girls, who became excited as I told them of all the wonderful things God has done in my life. I asked if they knew of a church where I could share my testimony, for tomorrow was Mother's Day, and I knew by the Spirit that I was supposed to speak to hurting mothers. Wanting me to go to their church to minister to their congregation, we made arrangements to meet in front of the hotel at 9:30 the next morning, and they would pick me up.

That evening, I went back to the hotel to have dinner with my friends. After I finished eating, I told them it was time for me to go to work again. When I saw their puzzled looks across the table, as if to ask me what I meant, I responded by quoting a thought from Rev. Norval Hayes, who said that if you don't give out tracts, cast out devils, and win souls, then he doubts whether you are saved. Not wanting anyone to doubt my salvation, I got up, took my tracts, and started giving them to everyone in the dining area and bar.

Tracts are very much an instrument in aiding me to win souls, and minister in miracles, signs and wonders. This is especially the case with hotel lounges, bars and restaurants and on beaches, because it seems as though I have met more interesting people that way, and some are my best friends to this day. Perhaps some may question why a Christian would go into the bars and restaurants. The Word of God declares, in Romans 10:14, *"How then shall they call on him in whom they have not believed? and how shall they believe in him of whom they have not heard? and how shall they hear without a preacher?"*. I sincerely believe that people in these places would not necessarily walk into a church, nor attend an evangelistic crusade, but they need to hear about the love of God. After all, you may be the only Bible some people read, or the only voice of God they hear. Faith comes by hearing, and it is the goodness of God that converts the soul. Jesus went and spent time with the publicans and harlots, and was accused of being sacrilegious. To "whomsoever will" comes the call of God; so we must go out, find them, and compel them to come in.

As I handed out tracts to people, some would ask me what it was about. I would smile at them and say, "It is about Jesus, and how much He loves you. He loves you so much that He died for you. If you don't want to read it now, you can take it to your room and read it later." Most people were kind and thanked me; however, there were also those who mocked me, but that didn't bother me. I have learned not to take offense at these things, for *"Great peace have they which love thy law: and nothing shall offend them"* (Psalm 119:165). For me, I just keep on tearing down the devil's kingdom, winning one soul at a time.

5

Do Not Pass Me By

Eternity if forever

One man observing me for a little while finally came to introduce himself, telling me he was from Holland and was on vacation. Influenced by New Age beliefs, he stated over and over, "You have the power to bless people, don't you?" I said, "Yes, sir, I do." He told me that he had brought a friend with him, who was given up to die. Showing great concern, he asked me, "Will you please go and visit my friend, and tell him what you are telling us?" There were many times in the Word of God when people would come up to Jesus and ask for help, and He would respond by going. He cares for each and every burden we have. So I went, and to my surprise, he introduced me to a very dignified elderly gentleman who was noticeably prominent, but appeared to be greatly disheartened.

My heart was moved with compassion, and I stood for a moment considering the wonderment of God. How often do we miss the opportunities given to listen to the heart of God, to go into the highways and byways? Are we willing to go to the places of both the humble and the affluent? This wealthy man on the outward perception would not give the appearance of desperation, but issues of the heart know no barrier of culture, nativity, race or social status. This man was fighting for life, love and freedom from rejection. He was full of questions about the reality of a caring God. Thus we talked about the differences between Christianity and other religions.

I proceeded to tell him that other beliefs offered a form of religion, but Jesus Christ is the only God who offers salvation. Christianity is different because it is based on a relationship with the person of Jesus Christ, instead of on observing empty rituals. What Jesus did as God and man, was that He died in our place for our sins. By shedding His blood, He took upon Himself our guilt, making us not only forgiven, but also making us new inside. When people are searching for the defining reason that separates our God from the pretense of lesser gods, the reality of dwelling in Heaven or hell for eternity becomes a key factor. When I began to call this man to account for his ultimate decision to choose the living God and determine his eternal fate, that is when the fear of the Lord became his wisdom. You could feel the weight of those words sink in. As I told him about God's wonderful plan of salvation, he prayed the sinner's prayer and gave his life totally to Jesus Christ. That man's life was truly hanging in the balance with not many days left on earth, but his decision altered the course of eternity for him.

As the young man who brought me to his friend listened intently, he was captivated by the power of the Gospel. I turned toward him and said that the Lord still moves in signs and wonders, and that God would give him a miracle to persuade him to believe in the one and only true God as well. He was a seeker of the supernatural, for there are many out there who are looking for a sign. Some collect crystals, and some call out to self-proclaimed clairvoyants who prognosticate the state of affairs. It is Jesus alone who makes known the truth, for God knows the end from the beginning as it has been established since before the foundation of the world. Only Jesus has the true authority to move in signs and wonders; He parts the sea, He heals the sick, He moves in glory and manifests in the supernatural. I saw God move on this young man and told him to look in the mirror to see what I saw, and determine for himself that God is still moving in signs today. As he looked in the mirror, to his amazement, he truly saw. Like a cloud of glory, the golden dust of beauty transformed his countenance, and as he asked, God faithfully responded, and now he knew no other could match His treasured worth. The presence of God filled the room in unusual signs that astounded both men, and confirmed the reality of the miracle working power of God that still exists today.

Their lives were forever changed that day because I made a choice to pass out tracts in a bar. Little do we know the impact or significance a simple Gospel tract will have when a hungry soul hears or reads of the Good News of Jesus Christ. So affected by that evening's event, the young man called my hotel room early the next morning, thanking me for miracles I had given them both. I told them it was my pleasure to win souls and I was just an instrument God uses; however, I could not give anyone miracles, for only Jesus performs miracles.

Another miracle. What an awesome God!

6

A Divine Connection on Mother's Day

Still rejoicing over the previous night's events, I was looking forward to meeting Joyce and her friends to attend their church and speak for the Mother's Day service. I waited in front of the gate of the hotel to have my ride pick me up; however, at ten o'clock I was still waiting. As time passed, I became more anxious and started praying. I told God that I knew He wanted me to speak on Mother's Day, because I knew that I had a testimony as great as any mother's, and that it needed to be heard to encourage mothers to never give up praying for their children, no matter how bleak the situation appeared. It did not matter if their children were born with deformities, or if they were on drugs or alcohol, or if they were bound by any other sin. I beseeched the Lord, "Lord, I know You want me to give this testimony, but to whom do You want me to give it? The church has not come with my ride." I remember how I stood there crying, reminding the Lord how I had fasted and prayed for direction from Him and without a doubt I was supposed to share this testimony with His people on Mother's Day. I was weeping and, suddenly, I started to groan in the Spirit as the Bible speaks about, in Romans 8:26, *"But the Spirit itself maketh intercession for us with groanings which cannot be uttered."* It was then that I knew I had touched the throne room of God. In other words, my answer was on the way.

As I was praying, people dressed in fine apparel began to come in through the gates of the hotel. I wondered if they were going to a church service, but one man in particular caught my eye. He was a very tall man, who was dressed like a preacher, and you could actually feel the presence of God radiating from him. I later came to find out that his name was Rev. Rhoan Matheson, so I approached him and inquired if he knew of a church service planned nearby. He said that there was indeed a service planned, which was being held in the banquet room of the very hotel I had been staying in for Mother's Day. Unbeknownst to me, I was speaking to the man who was to be the guest speaker. I shared some of my testimony about my life, and about our mission trip, and I inquired if he thought I might be given the opportunity to testify. Further explaining that we had come in from ministering in the bush country, I felt an urgency in the Spirit to share my testimony and a message on prayer without ceasing. I also elaborated on the fact that another church was supposed to pick me up at the gates at 9:30 AM, but they never showed up. Very politely he said, "You are more than welcome to join us." Thankful for his kindness, I told him I would wait a few more minutes for the people to pick me up, and if they didn't come, I would join this service. My ride never showed up, so I went back into the hotel and then entered the banquet room.

In the banquet room, there was an assembly of approximately two hundred people. Little did I know that this was the meeting, and these were the ministries, who would be the divine connection prophesied by Thelma, my friend, before the trip. As I walked into the room, I could feel the mighty presence of God with the worship so intense, all I could do was lift my hands to Heaven and worship the Lord. The glory of the Lord was surely in that place. In front of the room was a beautiful banquet table for all the ministers representing various affiliated churches. Seated at the table also was the city councilman of Montego Bay. As the music stopped, Rev. Mae Walker started welcoming everyone present, and then she started introducing the people at the banquet table, including the city councilman. To my surprise, she said, "We have another special guest here who came all the way from North Carolina. Evangelist Patricia Thomas, will you come up here and be seated at the banquet table with us? We want you to share your testimony."

Would you believe that not only was I going to preach and share my testimony, but I also was sitting at the banquet table? The same little woman who was outside crying waiting on her ride to come just a few minutes ago is now seated at the banquet table, with dignitaries and the city councilman of Montego Bay. You see, when the Lord hears your prayers and makes intercession for you, anything can happen. Within minutes of talking with my now dear friend, Rev. Pauline Knight, not only was I granted the opportunity to speak, but also I became the guest speaker. Months before, when this Mother's Day service was in the planning stages, I know that God foreordained who would be speaking on that day. Ironically, my ride did come; however, it was according to Jamaica standard time, which translates into thirty minutes or more after the actual time scheduled. They had just missed me, but if we had done things according to plan, I would have missed the divine connections and God's appointment for me to speak.

That morning, I had felt led to bring a framed picture of Patrice to display as

I shared my testimony. At first I addressed the mothers on Mother's Day about the high callings of motherhood, and the miracles God had performed in Patrice's life, which led into my Scripture text. There is no doubt in my mind that God ordained this Mother's Day service to be held in the very hotel where I would be staying and had prepared the way for me without my knowledge. I would not have been in a financial position to rent that glorious banquet room, or even known that I was actually going to stay in that very hotel. My Father, who owns the cattle on a thousand hills, provided everything I needed. Everything! I sat at the head table with the dignitaries of the community and was able to talk about the very passion of my heart: the blessing of being a mother, the blessing of having a daughter, and the blessing of knowing as a faithful husband God my heavenly Father. There was such a witness to the testimony that the people received the word of the Lord with shouts of joy and rejoicing.

After I had spoken at the banquet, they presented each mother with a special Mother's Day mug to commemorate the event, along with a beautiful rose corsage. In my heart, I felt that Patrice was in Heaven asking Jesus to make sure that I received a Mother's Day gift. Overwhelmed with gratitude when they pinned a rose on me and gave me a mug that said "Mom" on it, I could not stop weeping. After all, Patrice always made sure that I had a special card and a gift every Mother's Day. Those gifts meant more to me than I could ever imagine, especially now that my precious daughter was in Heaven.

It was at this very banquet that I met Peggy and David Whitehead, missionaries from Georgia, who were videotaping the service. After the service, they came and introduced themselves to me. Sister Peggy told me that she knew God had sent me there that day to encourage her. She told me about her precious grandson who had been born with autism, and that my testimony and sermon regarding praying without ceasing had influenced her so much, to never give up on praying for her grandson's healing.

Peggy and I started communicating on the telephone when I returned to the States. She told me about going with her husband to Jamaica several times a year, and that they especially had a heart for the girls at the girl's home. She continued about the different things they would bring to the children and about the needs of these girls, which touched my heart so greatly. I knew then that this would not be my last trip to Jamaica, and that I would make it a point to see the girls when I came back. Through the sequence of these events, at that Mother's Day service, I was able to make the right connections in Jamaica, paving the way for me to return and continue the mission work that was started. I was invited back by Rev. Pauline Knight to minister at a conference and in the surrounding churches in November of that same year.

Two years later, I would have the privilege and honor to minister at the Mother's Day service again. This time the crowd was larger than the first year I spoke. I was totally amazed at all the ministers and dignitaries seated with me at the banquet table. Would you believe that the honorable mayor of the city was there as well? When I think of where God had brought me from, and where He has brought me to, I stand amazed. If God can use someone like me, who can hardly talk, let alone speak before hundreds of people, what can He do for you?

I just want to address and encourage all the mothers who are reading this portion as God did for me, and comment on how special you are to all of humanity. As I looked back and considered all those beautiful mothers sitting in the room, my heart began to reflect on the beauty of motherhood, and how God created the affectionate care of a mother's love to carry us through life. This is for all the mothers who sit up all night with sick children, saying, "It's OK, honey; Mommy's here." This is for all the mothers who have their child innocently ask, "Did you see me, Mom?" to hear the reassuring voice of Mom say, "Of course, I wouldn't have missed it for the world." Moms have the special ability to hear the voice of their child call out "Mom?" in a crowd. The attributes of a good mother are patience and compassion. They have the ability to be multifaceted. They never lose their heart to love their child even when that child can be so unlovable at times. Mothers feel an ache in their heart when they watch their child grow up, graduate from school, or walk down the aisle to say, "I do."

Through the years and through the tears, we see our little ones transform from just potential to living possibility. To all you mothers who have lost a child, as I have, I pray for the grace of God to carry you through. You can face your future because of all the wonderful memories you made that give you strength. May we mothers be thankful to God for the rare and special gift He gave us that was truly our own personal miracle. By the Spirit of God, there is nothing that can take away the wonderful, giving and caring call of motherhood from us. Keep persevering, and know that God designed you to help shape and influence the world for His Kingdom, and you never know what great man or woman of God you will bring into the world to change the course of the world from history to "His story"! God bless you, precious mothers!

Another miracle. What an awesome God!

7

The Mission Fields

My Personal assignment

The mission field is a source of untapped destiny, where the miracle power of God not only worked for me personally but also would bring hope and life to the impoverished, the homeless, the hungry, the sick and the children. We were all created to serve with passion and receive God's "personal assignment" to fulfill the Great Commission. Reflecting on my trip to Jamaica, I began to understand more about my personal assignment. Although life was good to me back in the States, I was surrounded by reminders of that beautiful experience; days when it was humid and the fragrance of certain flowers transported me back to Jamaica and I began to long for Jamaica again.

It is easy to take for granted the luxuries and conveniences in America, where there are a great variety of churches on every block, controlled climate, and comfortable pews. Many of us are satisfied with a form of religion, and we reassure our consciences by attending the church of our choice every Sunday, with predictable routines and an array of close friends. Intellectual assent to Christian principles does not mean that we have obtained the truth or have arrived. It is difficult to leave the comfort of our homes to serve in local community projects to help the less fortunate, let alone go to another country where the conditions are destitute. The reality is that seventy-five percent of the world's Christians live in the Third World nations. Often the minority religion, they suffer persecution and are discriminated against. They are treated as second-rate citizens, only because they were born in countries that are predominant Hindu, Buddhist or Muslim.

We must all respond to the call of the Great Commission, for Jesus asks us to do for others. We come to God asking what He can do for us, but most of us don't ask what we can do for God. Are we willing to give up everything? Do we long to be in His presence, cultivating an intimate relationship with God? Will we love God instead of just having a friendship with the Lord? Will people know that we are believers, and even Christians, by the love we show and the things we do?

My personal assignment has been to go to the nations and bring the Good News, especially to the children. These abandoned lives are important to God for the reason that they are starved for attention and someone to acknowledge them. It doesn't take great accomplishment to hug these children, just someone who is "willing." In light of my journey to the mission fields, I am now praying for an open door where I can be a mother to the orphans for at least a year. It is my heart's desire to minister to them for a year on a daily basis, but until then, I am being sent to many places, so I do the best I can when I am with them. There is no greater value received than to see their little faces light up with smiles that warm your heart when you tell them that they are beautiful, for that is how God sees them.

When I go to the mission field, I don't just minister to church congregations. I go to the highways and byways, to the souvenir shops and witness to the owners, to the bars and restaurants of the hotels and win them to Jesus Christ. Every day I am with teams of believers who are ministering salvation in the streets, holding revivals, and praying for the sick. We see thousands of souls coming to the saving knowledge of Christ. I had already experienced divine appointments, meeting strategic leaders on my first trip to Jamaica, and I knew that there would be more yet to come.

Working in the mission field is a privilege. When you lay hands on the sick, and witness the glorious power of God minister to the masses of humanity, healing cancer, bringing salvation, and demonstrating full deliverance from demonic oppression and possession, there is no experience that can compare. No matter where you go, the universal language that connects us all is worship, for it brings hope and allows us to take flight above the storms we face. It was in my journey here and then abroad, that I had become stronger, passing test after test. Now with true compassion and confidence, I would take my "personal assignment" and do only what the Father had commissioned me to do. I was ready to go back to the foreign soil of Jamaica, and begin to put into operation the things I needed to do.

8

Preparing for a Journey

Expanding My Faith

November was approaching, and I was making arrangements with Rev. Pauline Knight to speak at the upcoming convention. I mentioned about wanting to see the girl's home in Falmouth that Sister Peggy directed me to, which supported approximately eighty-seven girls who were in great need of many essentials. I had purposed in my heart that when I returned, I would visit the home to minister to the girls and give each of them a gift bag. Rev. Pauline, pleased with my plans, asked if I would consider offering gifts to the children in her church. In addition, she suggested for me to contact Rev. Mae Walker, one of her close affiliates, to provide gifts for their children as well. When I spoke to Rev. Mae Walker, I was already wondering how I would acquire gifts for the eighty-seven plus children. She was excited about the offer, but then I became overwhelmed, especially when I found out that she had about two hundred and fifty children. I understood the challenges of going to the mission field, but now my faith was really being stretched and I knew I had my work cut out for me. To play it safe, I would need about five hundred bags to accommodate all the children.

I think that it is imperative to know that one must be determined, if you ever want to be successful at anything, especially fulfilling the call of God on your life. You must not let anything or anyone break your focus, because broken focus is the reason many people fail and never complete their mission. Notice that the Bible declares, in Matthew 11:12, *"The kingdom of heaven suffereth violence, and the violent take it by force"*. Satan will use people to tell you all the reasons you shouldn't do what you are doing, such as in my case. An excuse might have been, "You don't have the money to go to other countries," or "Your health is not the best," or else "You could get killed over there; aren't you afraid?" However, the most common objection was, "How do you think you will get the money for the supplies and how do you think you're going to get everything there? My answer would be, "I will get these things by faith in God."

People would shake their heads, disapproving of me as though it would never happen, or maybe they thought I had taken my faith a little too far. Faith will take you to places where others fear to go, but the nature of faith is to make us strong, and God wanted to strengthen my faith. He wanted me to be a strong woman who wasn't afraid of anything, but who would show courage in the midst of all my critics. My thoughts were inspired by the story of Mother Teresa, who was determined to open an orphanage in India. At first, the Catholic Church was hesitant to help her, but that didn't stop her. They asked her how she thought she was going to build an orphanage, which was another way of implying that they would not help her. It was at that time that her faith had to rise like an eagle. Keeping in mind that she only had one penny, she stated, "With one penny and God, I can do anything." I knew that if Mother Teresa could open an orphanage in India with that type of faith, it would be possible for me to complete my mission as well. The Bible states in Philippians 4:13, that we can do all things through Christ who strengthens us.

It is a fight of faith all the way, but if God gives you a vision to do so, you can't listen to anyone. If doubt plagues your mind, you will die without ever fulfilling your destiny on earth. Determination in God will help your faith rise like an eagle. Your faith has to soar above your circumstances, your family and friends, as well as your enemies. I was determined to take five hundred bags of treats to the children with Bibles, soap, washcloths, toothpaste, toothbrushes, underwear, shampoo and bundles of candy.

Everywhere I went, I told people of my need, inviting them to help me bless the children of Jamaica, and many responded. I also wrote letters to a few companies that made linens, telling them of my mission and asking for donations. Donations of more than five hundred bars of soap came as well as many items to be included in the gift bags, which came from various friends. A small pharmacy donated items, and a local textile company responded to my letter by sending one thousand washcloths to my house. Grocery stores donated powdered fruit punch, while with monetary gifts, I was able to purchase one thousand cookies.

These children are raised on rice and beans and very seldom get the opportunity to enjoy the luxury of treats like these. It is a special blessing for these children to receive a gift and have a little party, and they are so grateful. The most important thing I could give the children, however, was the Word of God, because that would be the enduring gift that would alter their lives and bring everlasting hope to them. A special blessing came from my friend Rev. Thelma Wilkins, who provided five hundred plus full-sized Bibles, enough to give one to each child.

After receiving all these wonderful items, I needed a place to organize all of the supplies to assemble the gift bags. My gracious employer let me store all these items in his stockroom. He also allowed me to take time off work to minister to the people. I thank God for an understanding Christian employer who would rather put God first and allow me to work for the Lord.

By this time I had received just about all the items I needed except for shampoo. With God, He is concerned with every detail. A week before I was scheduled to leave, my girlfriend Bobby took me to lunch to inquire about things I needed for the trip. Well, you know my favorite saying, "God's always on time, but seldom early." She told me her husband was very good friends with Van Stamey, who owned a shampoo plant in Kannapolis, North Carolina. She then called her husband and arranged for us to meet with Mr. Stamey. Upon meeting him, I found him to be a very kind man and was able to really share my heart about the missions and the great needs the children had. I explained that we had made gift bags with treats and necessities for the children, and that we had everything except shampoo. When he asked how many bottles of shampoo I would need, I was afraid to tell him at first, but then I spoke up and said, "I will need five hundred bottles." Another miracle happened when he said, "Give my workers time to box it up and get it ready for you." My heart was overwhelmed with joy; I was so astounded that this man, whom I had just met, had such a giving spirit to help the little children.

Two nights before my scheduled departure, my friends and fellow workers volunteered their time to help me pack all of the supplies according to the airline standards that could not exceed seventy pounds. We formed an assembly line with each person placing an item in a bag until it was completely full, sealed, and placed in a box for transport. Over twenty-two seventy-pound boxes were filled and loaded into a truck. Looking back on each and every miracle to get me to this point, I was amazed at the faithfulness of God. I did not realize how much there was to pack, but there was absolutely no lack.

I borrowed my friend's pickup truck, but there were so many boxes that the truck was overloaded. When I arrived home, I was totally exhausted and it was late at night; however, I checked my mail, and to my surprise, one of my friends had sent me a check for one thousand dollars. In the note she wrote about watching Trinity Broadcasting Network, and as they were asking people to pledge one thousand dollars for their telethon, she looked at her husband and said, "I am going to make the pledge, but I am pledging it to Trish." She told him she heard my spirit crying out, "Lord, I need help, and I need the money to pay for the expenses of getting all these Bibles and supplies over to Jamaica."

You probably wonder why in the world I went ahead and packed all the items if I didn't have the money to send them. Again, I'll remind you what the Word declares, in Hebrews 11:1, *"Now faith is the substance of things hoped for, the evidence of things not seen."* I have that "now faith," and I don't know any other way. I feel God speaks to us individually in a language we understand. I understand faith, and you might understand something else, but I hope by the time you finish reading this book, you, too, will understand my language.

9

Terminal Blues or Terminal Faith

After getting the truck back on the hill and opening my mail, I was so tired. I did not concern myself about anything. My body ached from the day's work, so I went home and fell into a deep and peaceful sleep. When I awoke, my friends Curtis and Celeste Montgomery took into consideration my dilemma and rented a U-Haul truck to transport the boxes to the airport. So relieved that I did not have to drive the overloaded truck to the Charlotte Airport, I saw that things were going better than expected, but I had not come upon the last obstacle yet. When I arrived at the airport, I met up with Noreen, who would accompany me on this trip to Jamaica.

Making arrangements to have my boxes taken to the boarding location, we stood in long lines waiting our turn to check in. Taking the precaution in advance to check on airline standards, I was assured that as long as the boxes did not exceed seventy pounds there would not be any problems. However, when I was ready to check in, I was shocked when the ticket agent notified me that the cost of the extra boxes would be in excess of three thousand dollars! It was like time stood still for a moment, a place where you stand alone with God and contend for your faith. My mind reflected on the words of Brother Love who would see me operate in great areas of faith. He said, "Sometimes, sister, your faith works so greatly that some people would mistake you for being insane, but I know that you have a true gift of faith!" It was at this time that I was beginning to understand what Brother Love said; I could relate to what he said. Have I totally lost it? What makes me think that I can get all these boxes over there anyway? But then I thought about the children, and began to pray for a miracle. I thought, *Well I have a choice here, to turn around and go back home; nevertheless, these Bibles have the potential of winning millions of people to the Kingdom of God. If we can get them into their hands, we can raise soul winners, even if it costs every penny I have.* Therefore, I would have to be successful because of all the souls that would be saved. Suddenly, I remembered where I was, and there was a long line of people behind me. I had to regain my composure and move forward.

Attempting to negotiate a more reasonable concession, I explained at length that these boxes contained items for the Jamaican children in need, and that they were for charitable purposes. The agent was unable to change the terms, so I located the credit cards in my purse. I split the cost between two debit cards, depleting both ministry and personal accounts along with one regular credit card to cover the cost of shipping. The Bible challenges us to count the cost, and to me souls are more valuable than my monetary assets.

I did not come this far to turn back now, and I was on my way to see the children. I was going to take them treats and make sure they were still following in the footsteps of Jesus, and I knew that nothing would stop me. I had no alternative but to accept and understand their position. It felt like I waited for hours, but as I stood in the airport, I wasted no time, sharing the Gospel with travelers, clerks and anyone else who was interested. I prayed for guidance and direction. My money was gone and the credit cards were charged to the limit, but I was on board my flight at last.

Another story related to this miracle of faith was how God provided for my expenses when I returned from this particular mission trip after spending everything I had. Two nights before leaving Jamaica, Noreen reviewed my bill from US Air and noticed a discrepancy. She told me I was overcharged for services and encouraged me to contact US Air to discuss the items in question. After I spoke with a representative, they concurred on the error, and credited the difference to my debit card. Praise God! Those funds enabled me to pay for my hotel accommodations and I felt as though one thousand pounds of pressure was lifted off of me.

When I returned home, a friend of mine approached me and said, "Trish, I bet you had to spend a lot of your own money to pay for the boxes to be transported to Jamaica. How much did it cost you?" I said, "It was around three thousand dollars. It cost me everything I had, but I wouldn't trade the experience of that mission trip for all the money in the world. If I had to do it all over again, I would." Visibly moved by my response, my friend asked me, "What is the name of your ministry?" I responded, "Faith Works Ministries." The next day, they handed me a check in the amount of three thousand dollars. What a mighty God!

In your journey of life you will be confronted with many Mount Moriah experiences like Abraham, the father of our faith. It was on Mount Moriah that Abraham was challenged to offer up Isaac, his son, as a sacrifice. It was the ultimate test of faith and love for God. It is when you pass that test that God will meet you on the other side with the provision. As Abraham was walking up one side of the mountain with his son and a willing heart, he trusted God with everything within him. At the same time that sacrificial ram of provision was walking up the other side of the mountain. God will be there to meet you with provision just like He was for Abraham on Mount Moriah. If it cost nothing, then it would not be a sacrifice. You would never have the privilege to experience the faithfulness of God and see His miracle-working hand move in power for you.

Another miracle. What an awesome God!

10

The Open Door

When we landed in Jamaica, my heart was full with the feelings of seeing family again, precious relationships that I had missed so much. Overwhelmed with joy, I knew that soon I would be able to see all the beautiful children. I still had to deal with customs in Jamaica that wanted to charge additional taxes on our gifts. I didn't want anything called into question; therefore, I contacted Rev. Pauline Knight to come to the airport to help me explain my situation. Since we arrived earlier than scheduled, she came as quickly as she could. She is recognized and respected by the Jamaican people and oversees many churches and missions, so when she arrived, the customs officials let us right through.

Packy, whom we saw a lot of, was Reverend Pauline's driver. He took us to the hotel, and immediately after we dropped off our bags, we went off to the first conference to minister. The schedule in Jamaica was full, with various conferences, church ministries, street witnessing and parties for the children. The expectancy was great to see what God was going to do. A significant part of our time was spent driving to meetings, which would take at least forty-five minutes minimum to get us from place to place. Also, the weather was very hot and the highways and bumpy roads made the trips long, but it was always worth it to see the Lord move and minister to the people.

Reverend Pauline's church was situated in the center of Falmouth, which was right in the middle of the roughest part of town where prostitutes and drug addicts congregate. Her church was an open-door type of ministry, where the breeze-ways made it easy for outsiders to observe. I had the opportunity to speak at many of her services as well as at Rev. Mae Walker's church in Canaan. One night while I was preaching, skeptics threw firecrackers at the church to sound like gunshots, attempting to shut the meeting down. Reverend Pauline leaned over to me to tell me that they were just firecrackers, but I was not afraid and kept preaching. The power of God was strong during that meeting, so that in spite of the opposition, countless people came forth for prayer and received miracles. It was wonderful to witness. In Jamaica, all classes of people meet together, from the richest to the poorest. They have a sound of worship that raises the roof with calypso rhythms unique to their culture. It is a sound that inspires me, for no matter where you are in the world, the presence of God always inhabits the praises of His people.

One night when I returned to the hotel and started passing out tracts to everybody, a middle-aged lady named Jill questioned me, "Oh, what's this about?" I proceeded to tell her that it was about how God loved her, and we began to talk some. She told me that she goes to church and was looking for a church while in Jamaica for her son's wedding. I casually invited her to go to church with me, and assured her that I could provide transportation. I did not tell her anything about being the guest speaker, or what part of town we were going to. After talking to her, I knew that she came from a Presbyterian background and that it was best not to concern her unnecessarily.

The next evening, we headed out for our forty-five-minute drive through the city and country roads to the church and then got situated in the sanctuary. You can imagine what she thought through the first part of the service as the worship started, but it only intensified when she saw me go up and speak. She looked as though she was in shock as her eyes gazed over the whole scene because of the differences in worship between the Pentecostals and the Presbyterians. However, as I began to minister, my testimony touched her heart and she began to open up. Upon giving the altar call, although hesitant, she was the first one to come up for ministry. When I came near her, I barely touched her and she fell out under power of God. Although she had never witnessed anything like this before and had no idea of the workings of a Full Gospel meeting, you would have never known by her response at the altar.

On the way home, she shared with us that she had never witnessed the real power and demonstration of the Holy Spirit like that before, but her life was changed forever. She thanked me for bringing her, and has kept in touch with me since that time. That experience was the landmark of a new life. Now, she is pursuing the Lord with all her heart, longing to find the place of fellowship that was as moving as the night she came to the powerful church of Rev. Pauline Knight's.

11

The Clock Strikes Midnight

Have you ever considered what happens at midnight? It is a time where the Spirit of the Lord moves in mighty ways. Samson took down the gates of the Philistines at midnight, Boaz discovered Ruth at midnight, The Bridegroom gave a shout at midnight and Paul and Silas praised God until the jail doors opened and their chains and fetters fell off. It seems as though when it is the darkest hour, the Spirit of the Lord broods over us and brings deliverance to the searching heart.

By divine appointment, I met a man who was searching for those chains to be released. Just like Paul and Silas who were cast into the inner prison with their feet held fast in the stocks, we find ourselves in places of darkness. Again our chains are issues of heart, and not always apparent on the outward . What do we do when we are in the stocks and chains of circumstances and the dungeon of difficulty? As I passed out a tract, this man had the insight to see the key to his freedom.

Bob Ksioszk was a practicing Lutheran and builder by trade who had just been exposed to the teachings of Joyce Meyer. He had just started buying her tapes to discover more about this thing that was stirring in him. On vacation in Jamaica, there he was waiting for his soda, trying to enjoy a few more days before he went back home to Wisconsin. The day he received a tract would be the day that he would start walking in that deeper journey. After finding out that I was a missionary, he began to ask me one question after another. Since it was late in the evening, I rescheduled to meet with him the next day to continue our conversation.

Noreen and I met with him the next evening and sat for several hours having church in the lobby. I tried to answer all his questions about being born again, water baptism, and the Holy Ghost baptism with evidence of speaking in tongues. Like a deer that pants for water, this man wanted to excel in his knowledge of God and held on to every word I said. He was being shaken, but not shaken in heart, because he was starting to trust God. After I led him through the sinner's prayer, I saw the change of countenance, I invited him to consider being water baptized that night, to which he replied with great excitement and a resounding "Yes"!

Since all the hotel pools were closed, I asked then if he would be willing to be baptized in the ocean instead. It was along about midnight on November 16, 2002, that I baptized Bob in the ocean of Montego Bay. It is times like these when ministry becomes most rewarding, when you see a transformation in someone's life. Like Joseph in the Bible, who after the long years of betrayal, suffering, then triumph, called his son Manasseh which means, "forgetting all my toil," God makes you forget your pain when life comes forth. When chains are broken and hearts are set free, there is no greater treasure here on earth! The presence of God was overflowing Bob's heart as he came out of the water with his hands facing toward the heavens. Praising God with tears filling his eyes. He stood in the water worshiping God for what seemed like hours, while Noreen and I worshiped in the spirit.

Since that day, I have continued to mentor and maintain friendship. Sending books on the baptism and gifts of the Holy Spirit, he has received much truth and is growing quickly in a mighty fashion. I have been so blessed watching the fruits of my labor develop. Today God is using Bob to win souls and bring the love of God in a greater dimension to many hurting people throughout his homeland. The shout of God came at midnight again, and this humble man from Wisconsin was revolutionized, proclaiming, "I am forever changed!" and that he was!

Another miracle. What an awesome God!

12

The Heart of the Children

A Special Birthday Gift From God

My greatest love on the mission field is visiting the children. Although I have tremendous compassion for the poor and for disabled people, I still have a special place in my heart for the children. Through my several trips to Jamaica, and Cali, South America, I continue to be overwhelmed with how these innocent little lives are cast away as insignificant and unwanted. Most of the wealth in these Third World countries is drug related, therefore it is the children who suffer. Jesus said, in Matthew 19:14, *"suffer little children, and forbid them not to come unto me: for of such is the kingdom of heaven"*.

We are God's hands and feet on this earth. It is easy to walk by and ignore the needy, but it could be any one of us. We have been born in a country that is prosperous, but we are not more special in God's eyes. It is not about human rights, but it is a privilege because of providence. This is the very reason that missions need to be supported. These children are our future, and the difference of knowing Jesus Christ can save a nation and bring hope for tomorrow; that is why I love to minister to the needs of the children. We give parties to show them love, and as we touch their lives by spending quality time playing with them, talking with them and holding them, they are greatly impacted. All they know is that the world thinks they are of no value, but to God they are deeply loved and He has a great plan for them. One such party is worthy of mention, because I was very moved by the personal touch of a loving, caring God who thinks no small detail is insignificant.

The girls' home in Grandville, Jamaica is a governmental institution for orphans, abandoned girls, and girls with discipline problems, who are considered outcasts of society, but I see them as the future of Jamaica. I thought maybe one of these children could be the next Mother Teresa, or Kathryn Kuhlman, or great prophet of God. Missionaries already provide clothing and gifts, and continue to teach them at the home encouraging them to be a respected part of their world. They are taught about God and taught that they can aspire to be whatever they want to be. My heart went out to these girls because they were someone's daughter or sister, maybe even someone's mother. We wanted to support the Gospel efforts being made, not only to bring these girls gifts, but most importantly, giving them all a full size Bible. I feel that everyone deserves a Bible, because it is the "roadmap to heaven."

Through a word of knowledge, the Lord let me know that a little girl in particular would have a birthday on the day of our visit. So in obedience to the Holy Spirit, I felt led to wrap one extra gift as a birthday gift, so that the dear little girl would receive two gifts instead of just one. After I spoke to girls that day, I then stated, "I believe that it is someone's birthday today, and I have a special gift just for you." As I asked her to come up and receive it, a little eight-year-old girl who had just recently lost her mother, shyly responded and walked up to the front of the room. As she was walking, all I could think about was how I no longer had a daughter to bestow a birthday gift to, and this child had no mother to celebrate her birthday. I was so moved that God loved me enough to allow me to stand in the place of her mother. I gave her a hug and said, "I understand that you have just lost your mother, and my daughter went to Heaven a few years ago, so you need a mother and I need a daughter." She looked at me in tearful amazement, and I continued, "Today, I am going to stand in the place of your mother and present this gift to you, because you are so very special." All the girls sang "Happy Birthday" to her. Later that day, many came forward to receive Christ after that special miracle.

Who knows out of those who came forward that day in response to a simple miracle, what they will become someday? They are the next generation of prophets and evangelists. Every time a life gets transformed, He becomes the Father of the fatherless, and destinies change. I am always amazed at how personal God really gets, because He truly cared when no one else did. I truly believe that He brought me all the way from America to show that little eight-year-old girl how much He loved her, enough to celebrate her birthday. So often, we think that miracles and the gifts of the Holy Spirit have to be extraordinary events, but God cares about every little detail, even the heartfelt desires of a little eight-year-old girl.

Another miracle. What an awesome God!

13

A Haven From Heaven for West Haven

It is easy to tell someone that Jesus loves them, but it is greater to show them by wrapping your arms around a hurting child and letting them feel the love of God working through you. It is a superior calling to be an active part of the Body of Christ. Sometimes the conditions are atrocious, but these precious children are God's children. He loves them and wants them to not only hear that they are loved, but also, feel the love of God, for they have emotional as well as tangible needs that must be met.

The place that touched me the most was West Haven Children's Home, which is an orphanage for severely handicapped children. We would never have heard of West Haven Children's Home, if it had not been for meeting Sheri, the maid at the Holiday Inn in Montego Bay. While she was cleaning our room, Noreen, my roommate, told her we were missionaries heading to the girls home in Falmouth, and she suggested that we visit West Haven Children's Home. When Noreen told me about the orphanage, I said, "Noreen, we have given everything we have except one large bag of candy, and I don't even have the money to pay for this hotel when we leave in a few days. However, I feel a drawing in my spirit for these children, so I need to pray." Immediately, I got down on my knees beside my bed and cried out to the Lord: "Father God, in the name of Jesus, these little children we just heard about, have desperate needs for someone to come and visit them, and show them love. And Lord, I want to have a party for them just like the ones we had for the other five hundred children. Now I don't have any money, and they have needs; they need diapers, they need candy. I want to take them drinks, cookies and snacks, and I am going to have to pay for a ride to take us all the way out there. Lord, these are not my children; they are Yours. If You will make a way for Noreen and me, to get the money to go, I promise You I will go and show them all the love that is within me. Suddenly, the Spirit made intercession for me with "*groanings*" which cannot be uttered, as Romans 8:26 states.

It was at that time that I knew I had touched the throne room of God. When I got up from my knees, I said, "Noreen, the Lord is going to make a way for us to see these children." We left our room and went downstairs into the lobby where we ran into "Bob the Builder", the man that I had baptized the night before. Excitedly, he approached us and acknowledged that while he was praying for our ministry, he felt led to give an offering of $250. This was the miracle we desired; now we had enough to pay for travel expenses to and from West Haven, supply all the things that we needed to take to the children, and have a party.

West Haven Children's Home is an orphanage that facilitates the care of severely handicapped, both mentally and physically as well as psychologically disturbed children. Some of these children have been abandoned and found in garbage dumpsters or left on the steps of the orphanage itself. With six cinder-block buildings, each building is considered a "ward." The condition of this orphanage was so appalling that it is hard to express the emotions I felt as I entered the complex. There was a sea of faces. Some were just normal-looking children while others who were bedridden had adult-looking faces, except their bodies were the size of infants. Some beds had no sheets while others did, some had diapers while others were scantily clad in towels pinned as mock diapers, and unsanitary conditions were being attended to as well as possible by the workers. The children were starved for attention, and when we brought them candy, chips, juice and diapers, they were so happy to see us, they were screaming and jumping up and down. My heart was to make sure I hugged and kissed every child, so that not one would be left out.

One little boy in particular named Kevin walked with a limp but couldn't talk. From the moment we walked in the door, this little boy hung on to me for dear life. Although he couldn't talk, it was apparent that he understood everything. The Lord sent me a "little angel" to take me by the hand and lead me to each room where all the children were placed. Since he heard me say that I didn't want to miss anybody, he would point to things for me to see, and make happy noises when we would give gifts and party with each child. It was important to visit every area and living quarter of the children that were bedfast. Kevin made sure to take me to one child in particular even at the reprimand of his caretaker. This little boy was isolated from the others because of disorderly behavior, and had both hands tied to the bed. This caused my heart to be terribly saddened to see this little boy confined to the bed in such a cruel manner. Oh, how I wished I could rescue them. My heart longs for the day when the power of God is so strong that we as Christians can just walk through these places of torment, and as we walk by their little beds, the power of God heals and restores these young people. So that they walk out of there whole, dancing and singing praises to the Lord. But for today, I was doing the best I could. It was truly moving to see these little, helpless, deformed children respond and smile when they were told that they were beautiful.

The Bible says that children are a gift to us. When I reflected on the extreme needs of these children, I would remember how Patrice, my daughter, would cry out for the attention of her father. Realizing that these children not only were fatherless but they were without the love of a mother as well. It would reinforce that no matter what, even if it was for one or two days, these children deserved to have joy while on planet earth. I was consumed with the pain of thinking that a mother would desert precious gifts like these children. It was hard to pull away from the very children for whom I had such great compassion. Weeping, as we drove back to the city, I purposed in my mind that I would return someday soon.

Kevin, my little tour guide, kept taking my hat off and putting it on his head. My heart is to someday get little Kevin home with me, for he became one of my own little boys, a son to love along with the other little boy, Did of Chester Castle. On my third trip to Jamaica I was able to come back to see my little Kevin, give him the hat and other special gifts just for him. Each time I visited, I would try to take as many people as I could to share the love, regardless of their conditions or illnesses. It was important to touch them. It is a known fact that if a child has a tangible gift to hold on to, it will give them security. So on the next trip, I was able to bring little teddy bears that were prayed for and anointed before being given to the little children. Each time I went there I was better equipped to bring specific things that they needed.

This type of work is not one of the most popular facets of ministry, but it is definitely one of the more rewarding ones. In Heaven, when all us will be totally whole, even the handicapped children in the orphanages, these children will walk up to us and say, "I remember when you came to visit me in the orphanage." What an awesome eternal reward that will be.

Another miracle. What an awesome God!

14

People Really Do Care

Hotel Managers, Merchants and Team Ministry

By the time I went on my last trip to Jamaica, I was more seasoned and better prepared. Prophet Jimmy had a team going to Chester Castle, and I had a team going with me to minister with Pauline Knight at the Mother's Day service and visit the orphanages. Sister Eve Barker would be my roommate and team member along with Bob Ksioszk; both were armor bearers on our ministry team. These two mighty warriors held my hands up the whole time we were there. In the morning, Eve and I would pray, read the Word of God, and dance before the Lord while Bob would bring us coffee.

We brought so many gifts for the children from America that we had to store it all in Bob's hotel room. One particular night we all started packing the bags for the children, then Eve and I finally got so tired that we had to go back to our room and get some sleep. Bob stayed up most of the night and packed the rest of the bags. I am strong when it comes to ministering the Gospel, but when it comes to packing, my body weakens after several hours of hard work. To our surprise, when Eve and I got up the next morning, Bob had every bag packed and assembled. Needless to say, we were both very thankful.

On the previous trips I had also taken cookies and drinks, but this time after buying all the other items for the children, my finances were exhausted. I told Eve and Bob to leave me totally alone in my room; I had to get alone with God. Many times when I pray, I just want to be intimate with the Lord, just Him and me, for He is mine and I am His; I love my times alone with Jesus. Nothing can fulfill me like being in the presence of the Almighty King.

While I was alone in my room worshiping the Lord, I thanked Him for all the many blessings He had bestowed upon me, and thankful for allowing me the opportunity to minister to the orphans in Jamaica one more time. I had many things to bring to the children, but, I still didn't have any cookies or drinks for the party. Suddenly, I started weeping uncontrollably, as I was thinking about the precious children. The Holy Spirit started to make intercession for me just like He has many times when I prayed for the needs of His people. It was at that time that I knew that I had touched the throne room of God. I went down into the lobby where Bob and Eve were and I explained to them what had happened. I said, "I am going to visit the merchants at the souvenir shops that I had previously met, and tell them about the orphans and the rest of their needs. I feel that they are going to help, so here I go."

The storeowners all remembered me. Most of them were from India and many of them had given their lives to Jesus, as I had witnessed to them on some of my previous trips. It all happened so quickly. They were so very kind, and each shop owner gave me nice tee shirts to take to the children. The last store I went to, the owner looked at me and he asked, "What else do you have need of?" I was surprised; I was walking in the favor of God. I said, "I have about two hundred children, and I need a drink for each one of them. I can use diapers, and I need about four hundred cookies so they can have about two apiece for their party." He said, "I will try to get diapers, and will have the drinks delivered to your hotel room tomorrow evening."

I was so excited that I ran back to the hotel and called Rev. Pauline Knight to tell her about all the gifts. We also had nice tee shirts for all the children to wear, which were more than enough, and drinks from the kind storeowner's donation. She recommended for me to contact the hotel manager to ask if I could use their cooler to store the drinks, so that they would be cold for the children. Upon her suggestion, I went down to the lobby to talk with Dahlia Walker, the hotel manager. After I explained everything, she said she would be more than glad to accommodate the need. I could sense the presence of God coming over me similar to waves; it was like standing in the glory of God. She then asked, "Do you have any other needs?" I told her I needed rice and beans and about four hundred cookies. She said she would provide the rice and beans, and since Saturday was her day off, she would be more than glad to go to the orphanage and help us with the children. She then gave me the phone number of the general manager of the hotel, and told me to call him to explain my situation. She thought he would probably donate the cookies. Would you believe he donated four hundred freshly baked homemade cookies? The Lord is on my side!

I was now ready to explode with joy and shout the victory. Later that night after dinner, I started handing out tracts at the bar and restaurant. I met this wonderful couple from England, John and Rose, who were on their vacation. They started asking questions, to engage in conversation. So I explained to them that I was an evangelist and a missionary. I invited them to come to the Mother's Day service where I would be speaking. Then I told them about the orphanages, the condition of the children, and how they were in dire need of affection for people to go see them. They seemed interested, so I continued by telling them that we had all the supplies. Now all we needed were people to volunteer their time and visit with the children as an act of compassion. I invited them to come with our team to show them love, help give out the supplies, and feed the ones who could not feed themselves. They said they would be delighted. I was totally amazed that such new acquaintances who were very prominent retired people would take their vacation time, all the way from England, to help me share the love of God with these children.

It was early Saturday morning and the big day had finally arrived. Rev. Pauline Knight, her driver Packy, and another driver arrived at the hotel to pick us up. Waiting in the lobby, we were all ready to go; Bob, Eve, Dahlia the hotel manager, her friend, John and Rose, and of course, myself. What an awesome team God put together to bless the children along with the rest of the team coming from Chester Castle. It was a glorious time and the children were overwhelmed with joy when they saw us coming. I wish you could have been there with me to see the smiles on their faces. It was such a beautiful sight to behold. On our way back to the hotel, John and Rose told me that it was the highlight of their vacation.

Another miracle. What an awesome God!

15

On The Road Again

It had been a year since I was last on foreign soil and had just pulled through some very severe health challenges of my own. During that time I had a visitor come through who then was invited to speak at one of my home meetings. Encouraging the hearts of all those who listened that night, Prophet Nathan, a missionary with a heart for the people of South America, shared of his experiences on the mission field. I too was deeply moved as I reflected over my past mission trips and the many miracles that took place here and abroad. Isaiah summed it up so well in chapter 43:2, when he wrote, *"When thou passest through the waters, I will be with thee; and through the rivers, they shall not overflow thee: when thou walkest through the fire, thou shalt not be burned; neither shall the flame kindle upon thee".* I could look back and see the countless times that God had brought me through the rivers of peril and fires of adversity. My life had been greatly enhanced by these life-changing experiences and I was stronger because of the tests of life.

I was deep in thought, as his words filled my heart; I had come to love the mission fields more than ever. Traveling around the world winning more souls to the Kingdom of God, I could preach, teach and minister hope and love to everyone. My heart's desire was to be the best bride to Jesus and greatest mother to children all over the world. I wanted to shower them with love even if it's only for a few weeks, however long my mission trips lasted. When you go into these countries, the people are so grateful for anything you do for them. They love hearing about Jesus and they especially love when you pray for them. They receive miracles instantly because their hearts are so tender, and their spirits are so meek. If you give them a Bible, or soap, or even candy, they are so appreciative for everything, no matter how large or small. Since they have so little, seeing the smiles on their precious faces is worth it all.

As Nathan continued, something intrigued me regarding his next trip planned for Cali, Colombia, coming up in the next few weeks. He extended an invitation to join him and his team and encouraged us that anytime anyone ever accompanied him on a mission trip, God would use him or her in miracles, signs and wonders. In addition, he told us of the wonderful opportunity there would be to minister to and reach hundreds of children in Cali. Well, that caught my attention immediately, because I love children dearly and God uses me in miracles, signs and wonders. From that moment, I had a desire to go because I'm always praying, "God use me in the miraculous," and God always has. I thought to myself, "Well, I don't have any money, but money had never stopped me before." I also had suffered from severe health challenges that year, and most people in my physical condition probably would not have attempted to go on a foreign mission trip. However, I am not like most people. I am a strong woman of God who is not easily moved by my circumstances, especially when I know that it is God's perfect will.

The materials of the world can never take the place of God's love, and I am determined that, as long as I have life here on this great planet earth, I am going to use every fiber of my being to build the Kingdom of God. There is more to life than our immediate surroundings and circumstances. We must not get fixed on the things of this world or on obstacles, because they are not eternal. If we purpose in our hearts to worship Him, love our fellow man, serve others, and tell the Good News, we will ultimately become more like Christ. When I was a young girl, I wrote a poem that has become more real and meaningful as I have grown older and wiser, that went something like this:

> *Day by day I see people crying.*
> *Deep down inside I know they're dying.*
> *Why can't they see that materials*
> *Can never take the place of God's love.*
> *So come with me just like a dove,*
> *And with me I will show you love.*

You know by now my little saying, "If it's God's will it's God's bill." I knew God was leading me to go to Cali, Colombia, with Prophet Nathan and his team, so I prayed and fasted for God's direction and provision. Within a few days, somebody had sent me a check for $1500, which was more than enough to cover all my expenses. Again I can affirm that "God's on time, but seldom early," and thank God, He is an "on-time" God. Within two weeks, I was headed for Cali, Colombia, thanking the Lord for His provision and the opportunity to preach His Word again.

Another miracle. What an awesome God!

16

There Were Three Crosses

Cali, Colombia, is a huge city in South America with a population of approximately five million people plus. It is located in the northern west part of the country near the Panama Canal. There is a great need for revival in the city, which has earned the global reputation of having the second highest murder rate in South America. In addition to being the mainstream source of cocaine to the United States, it is the home of the infamous drug cartel mafia. Because of ruthless drug trafficking practices it has been difficult to deal with, requiring United States government intervention and protection agencies' involvement. There is also much persecution of the Christian church, with guerilla warfare and extremist groups killing Christian leaders and kidnapping American missionaries along with other innocent victims to exploit churches and their members for high profile exposure.

In a place like this, one wonders if God can bring change, but by divine intervention, God can transform this place and people of great darkness to hear the Gospel. When we understand that God has a passion for the lost, then we will weep with Him over the injustices. It is the Church that has to blaze this world with His glory, for light always overcomes the darkness. In spite of conditions, when the Spirit of the Lord sends you on a mission, no place is so untouchable that the grace of God cannot bring about change. There is nowhere His Spirit will not accomplish what He wills by our obedience. Psalm 118 declares, *"The LORD is on my side; I will not fear: what can man do unto me?"*. I have no fear when it comes to going on foreign soil, for this is an opportunity for God to display His glory. Although naturally shy, when I am ministering I become another woman, as Proverbs 28:1 declares, *"The wicked flee when no man pursueth: but the righteous are bold as a lion"*. I would rather die living a fruitful and productive life reaching as many souls for the Kingdom of God as possible, than live just existing in a noncommitted way.

There are characteristics that make us each individual, some of great strength and others that make us feel weak. As I said before, I am genuinely shy, especially when I am around very educated people. I talk slowly with a country accent, and at times I feel challenged to say things, which makes me feel self-conscious. But in Cali, Colombia, where the native tongue is Spanish, and all the ladies have long dark hair, I looked as though I was related to them, and with an interpreter, it was to my advantage to speak slower so that the interpreter could be more accurate in the translation.

Our small ministry team led by Prophet Nathan, included Prophet Abraham our interpreter, two women named Donna, Debbie and myself. When we first arrived in Cali that night, they lost our suitcases. Although all that I had were the clothes on my back, I did not care, because all I wanted to do was minister miracles, signs and wonders, and see the wonderful children! The next day our suitcases were recovered, and we were able to move forward as planned. In spite of that minor delay, I was still truly amazed at the fact that I believe God gave me the best room in the entire hotel. Nathan had made reservations in advance as part of our trip arrangements, but when I entered my room, it completely exceeded my expectations. It was an accommodation for royalty, large and beautiful, with windows overlooking the city all around. The bathroom was extremely large, having all the modern American conveniences along with a luxurious bathtub and a breathtaking view. Nevertheless, I was genuinely taken aback by what I noticed as I stepped up to capture the view from the enormous picture window. As I looked up from the valley to the beautiful hills surrounding my room, there lifted up before my eyes were three crosses illuminated in their entire splendor. Overcome with great heartfelt emotion and thanksgiving, I was reminded of the great sacrifice Jesus carried out as He died on the cross for me. I was the only one on the mission team who had such a view, and without a doubt, I felt at that moment that the Lord Jesus Christ Himself was smiling on me.

As I stood there viewing this majestic sight out my picture window, I began to weep. To think that God loved me that much, simply overwhelmed me with adoration and love for my Jesus, knowing that He cared so much for me. I was weeping and thanking Him over and over for such a beautiful view. I felt completely protected knowing that my Lord and heavenly husband would take care of me. He was faithful to show me that He was with me and would lead me each step of the way on this mission trip. Many times I have been comforted by Isaiah 54:5, which states, *"For thy Maker is thine husband, The LORD of hosts is his name, and thy Redeemer the Holy One of Israel; The God of the whole earth shall he be called."* For the remainder of that trip, every night I would look out my window before I called it a day, to see those three radiant crosses and behold that beautiful sight. Inspired by His presence, I would worship the Lord and thank Him for saving a wretch like me and giving me the great privilege to minister the Good News to the people of Cali, Colombia, South America.

Another miracle. What an awesome God!

17

By His Stripes We Are Healed

In the poorer areas of Cali, the pastors of the local area churches would accompany us as we would take nice bags of goodies to the poor and hold meetings in the streets during the daytime hours. As our team would start to pray, Nathan would play guitar and sing, attracting crowds by the hundreds. We would follow up by telling the people the plan of salvation. We told them how Jesus went to the cross, shed His blood to cleanse us from our sins, and became the Redeemer who heals us and save our souls. He didn't just come to die on a cross, but He was beaten for us with thirty-nine stripes so that we could be healed. While He stretched out His hands, the chastisement of our peace was upon Him, and with His stripes we are healed. The prophet Isaiah powerfully declared prophetically, in chapter 53:5, that our God was wounded for our transgressions and bruised for our iniquities. Many people were visibly touched and their hearts opened as the revelation of God's love was ministered to both young and old.

On foreign soil, many people not only suffer from impoverished situations, but are stricken with many untreated illnesses as well. So the message of a Savior who brings healing brings hope and great joy to those who suffer. I can only imagine how Jesus felt as He walked the streets two thousand years ago, facing the same predicaments, people lost and wandering in darkness who were in need of a touch from God. It moved our hearts with great compassion as we looked into the faces of these lost souls. We could see the chains of pain weighting them down, sicknesses beating them up, and broken dreams leaving them unfulfilled. There was a woman who had a debilitating cancer that caused her not to be able to walk for years. As Debbie and I prayed for her she was totally healed, and because of the blood that Jesus shed for her, she can walk to this day.

There were so many people coming up for healing that it is hard to count all the people who received healings and miracles during those times of ministering in the streets, but Jesus knew every heart and every soul. When the multitudes get saved and healed, God still loves them as individuals, knowing the number of hairs on their heads. He walks with them and talks to them. He agonizes with them as He intercedes in their place; He is the greatest High Priest ever offered for humanity.

An elderly woman who had severe sores on her ankles with pus coming out of them was standing in the crowd. Lost in thought momentarily, considering how great His love is towards us, I suddenly realized that I was the only one in the mission group who was not presently praying with anyone. Of all those who were standing on the street waiting for prayer, this woman's condition was the worst. It seems as though God always sends me to the critical situations. I thought to myself, *Lord, the doctors told me I don't have much of an immune system. What am I supposed to do God?* I had been diagnosed with some major health problems of my own, but I knew God had sent me to minister salvation, signs, wonders and deliverance to the people. So I resolved on my part to walk in obedience and do what the Scriptures exhort us to do: *"And these signs shall follow them that believe; In my name shall they cast out devils; they shall speak with new tongues; they shall take up serpents; and if they drink any deadly thing, it shall not hurt them; they shall lay hands on the sick, and they shall recover"* (Mark 16:17-18) . I went up to this precious woman, went down on my knees, and laid my hands on her feet. Most people would have been terrified to do this, given the woman's putrefying sores. Truthfully, I was a little apprehensive to lay my hands on her, but I did it that day, and would do it again!

At night we had miracle crusades. The pastors with their teams would build large platforms and place the chairs in open areas located near a church to facilitate crowds too large to come into the building itself. Nathan would preach at night while Abraham translated, and the ladies and myself would intercede. After Nathan's ministry, the intercessors would come to the platform to help pray for the people in miracle lines. There were many people Nathan had me pray for who were demonized. He would look for me and say, "Sister Patricia, we need you; we need you right now! This one is demonized….Minister to this woman….Come over here and pray for this person". Some of the people demonized would just go out in the Spirit with their bodies contorting in unusual ways, going down one way and coming up another. They were slain in the Spirit and going out under the power of God before you could hardly touch them.

During the services, I would sit with the crowd and interact with the children. When the worship and praise music started, I would get the children and have them hold each other's hands. Then forming a circle, we would start dancing round and round worshiping the Lord. Before you knew it, I would have hundreds of children in the circle just smiling. You could see their little eyes twinkle as their hope was renewed. I wanted them to know that it was a joy to serve the Lord. I wanted them to recognize that the Lord's presence comes when we rejoice, because He inhabits our praise. The children would now be able to see church as something joyful, instead of sitting in the service being bored. They could now interact by dancing and lifting their hands, worshipping the Lord with all their hearts.

It was quite a sight to see the whirlwind of children dancing, but in the corner there was one particular teenage girl who was just sitting there watching and mocking me as I intermingled with the children. Working in the ministry as long as I have, I was aware that it wasn't her heart to do this, but demonic spirits that were influencing her. The Holy Ghost revealed to me that she had been deeply hurt and wounded and that all she wanted was to be loved. When I kissed and hugged every child that I could see, that young lady would laugh, make noises, and make fun of me, but what she really wanted was to be a part of what I was doing with the other children. Later that week during the praise service, I walked over to her and her friend. They continued to show disrespect, but all I could feel was the absolute love of God for the two of them. It is important to be Spirit-led when you are ministering, because it would be easy to be offended and respond in anger. Jesus didn't judge people for what they were doing, but loved them unconditionally because He saw their future. He knew that teenage girl was called and ordained by Him, so I went over to her and felt His heart for her as I hugged and kissed her. The hard shell broke as I approached her and she began saying, "Oh, my God, here she comes, here she comes, she's coming to me. Oh, my God!" Even though we spoke different languages, that child could tell that someone genuinely loved her for who she was, unconditionally, no matter how mean she was and regardless of what had happened.

Because the crowd was so great on the platform, we dispersed many people to the nearby church and divided up into smaller teams to accommodate the need for more personal ministry. Donna and I and one of the in-house teachers took some people to a room in the church to pray and minister to the overflow crowd. To my surprise, the young teenage girl who had been mocking us came into my overflow room. As I looked at her in spite of our language barrier, the Holy Ghost revealed exactly what was happening in the young lady's life. The Lord showed me she had come from an abusive family, and as I relayed this through the interpreter, she started to cry. I explained the plan of salvation and said, "Now would you like to give your life to Jesus Christ?" She nodded her head and I asked her to pray and repeat after me. When I prayed, the interpreter translated and this precious girl would pray in her native language. As I continued, she fell out under the power of the Holy Ghost and God started showing me specific things through the word of knowledge regarding the abusive lifestyle of her home and family. She was weeping uncontrollably as the word of the Lord penetrated her broken heart. I could feel all the pain and turmoil this child had been through ever since she was born.

That night was a night of conversion for that young lady. Her entire countenance was altered from being mean-spirited to having her eyes radiate the love of God and exude the most beautiful smile. She didn't even seem like the same child. When you have an encounter with the living God, you are completely changed from darkness into His marvelous light. After that night of deliverance, she chose to sit beside me in the services every night hugging and kissing me. As we consider the multitudes, God still deals with us one person at a time, one nation at a time. It was His divine plan in the making of this young prophetess to completely transform her life. Only He knows what she will be one day. She may have had some previous religious experiences, but from that point on, she would have a real relationship with Jesus. He had passed by her, placing His mantle on her, calling her to serve Him and fulfill a great destiny. They told me later, after the last day of revival at that church, that she and all the children from that church brought fruit for me. Unfortunately, the Lord had led me to go preach at another church, so I wasn't there to receive their gifts. I was told that all the children cried because they didn't get to see me or give me their gifts. I was very honored by their love.

Many miracles took place as we prayed for people in the excess room, but there are always special encounters that become noteworthy to share. God moves in and through our circumstances to set us up for a miracle to be released. I started to pray for a beautiful lady standing in the prayer lines who had a tumor in her breast. As we prayed, she fell under the power of God and started telling the interpreter she felt this deep heat where the tumor was. Often, this feeling is a common experience among people who are experiencing the divine touch of healing. Very excited and grateful for our prayers, she believed that God had healed her. The next night she and her husband brought their little boy to the service and waited for me after the meeting ended. The interpreter told me that the little boy could not hear. As the people in the service were leaving the premises, I asked the boy's parents (through the interpreter) if I could pray for his ears. They said yes, and Donna ministered with me as I laid my hands on the little boy's ears to pray for the recovery of his hearing. I snapped my fingers on both sides of his ears and he started to nod his head with great joy. Salvation and healing came to the whole family that glorious night as he heard for the first time.

On Sunday, assignments were given to split the team and preach at the different churches. The Full Gospel Church I ministered to could facilitate a congregation size of around three hundred people, but because the crowds were so large, they had to hold several services one after the other. That morning proved to be a very wonderful time for me as I was scheduled to preach at 10:00 and 12:00. After preaching, I began ministering in the gifts of the Spirit with the anointing for discerning hearts and thoughts. Numerous people experienced the transformation of salvation, and the Spirit of God moved powerfully as almost all of the ones I prayed for fell under the power of God and experienced His loving touch.

Another miracle. What an awesome God!

18

The Unsung Hero

My story of my trip to Cali, Colombia, would not be complete if I did not tell you of one of the most precious woman I have ever met. She impacted my heart as she faced life with great courage and grace. I believe that God esteems those that others often miss. We often misunderstand people who are afflicted, or who do not fit our picture of someone we consider anointed. In that great day, when Jesus comes and judges our works, do we think that He will honor the great world evangelists more than the little prayer warrior who wins the multitudes in secret, as they pray and knock upon the gates of Heaven to see God move in the earth? It is a divine paradox to see who is strong and mighty in the Kingdom of God.

I believe that I met one of these people, in one of the most unexpected places of the world. Here in this infamous city of Cali, a woman who did not even speak the same language that I did had a faith that could move mountains. Rosalba de Zapata, mother of the Pastor, whose labor of love would change the world around her, interceded and prayed for the church before it existed. God heard the cry of this one righteous heart. She had earned the reputation of having signs and wonders follow. Many people received healing from this precious woman who spent hours in the presence of God, praying and believing. Even though we couldn't speak the same language, we had an immediate rapport and connection in the Holy Ghost. Pastor Nathan presented a picture of a medical doctor in Cali holding a big jar, of what appeared to be a massive stone, the size of a large baking potato. He continued to elaborate on how the doctor stated that this was nothing less than a miracle, but this man was healed by the prayers of this precious saint.

The real miracle, though, was that fact that Sister Rosalba de Zapata had an affliction that would have discouraged most anybody, except this woman. Rosalba was born with her feet backwards, instead of forward. Would you believe this precious lady prepared full-course meals for the entire ministry team every night, and even brought the food to the table? As I've stated many times, you can be pitiful or you can be powerful, but you cannot be both. This woman chose to be powerful for the Lord in spite of her handicap. Even though her feet were not what we call normal, she chose not to let her affliction stand in her way of being a powerful servant of God, strong in the Lord and in the power of His might. It has been said, "A strong woman works out every day to keep her body in shape, but a woman of strength stays on her knees in prayer to keep her soul in shape." The apostle Paul said he would rather glory in his infirmities, so that the power of God might rest upon him. Surely the power of God is resting upon this mighty woman of faith in Cali, South America.

The trip to Cali, Colombia, was rich and deeply moving, as we saw the power of God release the lives of many. As I have shared before, the mission field is a source of untapped destiny, where the miracle power of God works in the one who is sent to the field, as well as in those who are being ministered to. The message of the Good News is that Jesus died, shed His blood, and rose again to bring hope and life to the impoverished, the homeless, the hungry, the sick and the children. There is great joy given when we walk in obedience to fulfill the Great Commission, and there is nothing that gives a greater sense of accomplishment and fulfillment than to walk in obedience with God and see lives transform right before you.

Another miracle! What an awesome God!

Part 3

Conclusion

1

Forgive Them Anyway

Being an evangelist can be very challenging at times, with persecution that can be almost overwhelming. Many times I have cried so hard when people have persecuted and falsely accused me, that my tears flowed like a river. The pain of hurtful words at times is so intense that I actually feel as though I am crying tears of blood. I have such a heart of love for God and His people. All I want to be is of great service to the Lord Jesus and His precious people. For it is only the Lord who knows my heart, and really that is all that matters. I'm sure that many of my readers have felt the same kind of pain at times. So this is why I want to share this beautiful poem with you written by Mother Teresa, which is engraved on the wall of her Home for Children in Calcutta. It always brings me great comfort during my hard times to read this poem, and I keep this poem hanging on my wall, reading it over and over until my tears dry.

People are often unreasonable, illogical and self-centered;
Forgive them anyway.

If you are kind, people may accuse you of selfish, ulterior motives;
Be kind anyway.

If you are successful, you will win some false friends and some true enemies;
Succeed anyway.

If you are honest and frank, people may cheat you;
Be honest and frank anyway.

What you spend years building, someone could destroy overnight;
Build anyway.

If you find serenity and happiness, they may be jealous;
Be happy anyway.

The good you do today, people will often forget tomorrow;
Do good anyway.

Give the world your best and it may never be enough;
Give the world your best anyway.

You see, in the final analysis, it is between you and God;
It was never between you and them anyway.

2

Conclusion

In closing, I would like to share the purpose of writing *Miracles, Miracles and More Miracles*. The Lord impressed upon my spirit that many people would actually receive miracles, healings, deliverance and salvation while reading this book. Through this process, I have faced some of the hardest challenges in my life, and relived some extremely painful moments, but I was determined to finish this book to bring glory to God, not to myself. I found that the only way to get in touch with my destiny was to see the Lord, and trust Him to carry me where I could not go myself.

It is my heartfelt desire that your faith in God will grow exceedingly and that you will fall in love with Him more each and every day. My greatest aspiration is to win millions of souls to the Kingdom of God while the harvest is ready and the fields are ripe. May the testimony of my life and the accounts of those recorded, give hope to the hopeless, bring healing to the hurting and afflicted, and cause faith to arise in your heart for believing in the miraculous. Jesus Christ is still the same yesterday, today and forever. He is the same God who parted the Red Sea, turned the water into wine, and healed the lame, the blind, the sick and the afflicted. He is still the same miracle-working God today that He was two thousand years ago.

I would also like to say I am so very grateful for the gifts the Lord has bestowed upon me. However, more importantly, rather than just having the gifts of the Spirit, I have the *"Giver of all gifts,"* my precious Lord Jesus Christ, the lover of my soul and my dearest friend.

May God Bless You, With Much Love
Patricia Thomas

3

The Call of the Bride

Jesus, You are my very life
And that is why I've decided to be Your wife.
I long to see You face to face,
And because of this
I can't think of a better place.

I love to sing to You.
I love to dance with You.
I love to worship You.

You have been my Jehovah Jireh, my provider,
My Jehovah Rapha, my healer.
You are my cloud by day
And my fire by night.
You are my guiding light.

You are the lover of my soul,
And now I know
You have made me completely whole.
I love You dearly.
I believe Your Word,
And I understand it clearly.

Come, Jesus, come.

Written by Patricia Thomas
July 9, 2003

4

I Choose to Be a Champion

Losers focus on what they are going through.
Champions focus on where they are going to.

I know that someday Heaven will be my eternal destination. That is our ultimate goal as a believer in the Lord Jesus Christ. The Word of God declares, in John 14:6, *"Jesus saith unto him, I am the way, the truth, and the life: no man cometh unto the Father, but by me"*. To be a champion one must accept Jesus Christ as their Lord and Savior, repent of their sins, and ask Him into their heart. They too can make a choice to be a champion and focus on where they are going, because Heaven will be their eternal destination as well.

At this time I would like to invite you to take this opportunity to become a champion and give your life to Jesus Christ today. Romans 10:9 says, *"That if thou shalt confess with thy mouth the Lord Jesus, and shalt believe in thine heart that God hath raised him from the dead, thou shalt be saved"* .

Pray this prayer from your heart today!

Dear Jesus,
I believe that You shed Your blood on the cross
and died for me.
You rose again on the third day.
I confess that I am a sinner.
I need Your forgiveness.
Please forgive me of all my sins
and come into my heart.
I receive Your eternal life.

Congratulations, you are now a champion. Please let me know about your decision by contacting me on my website: www.patriciathomas.org.

The Ultimate Healing

Many are the plans in a man's heart,
but it is the LORD's purpose that prevails.
Proverbs 19:21, NIV

We thought the writing of the book was complete and had sent it off to the publisher. However, just as my dear friend Prophet H. B. Love told me from the beginning of this project, "You are going to have need for another miracle before this book is completed." In despair I replied, "Brother Love, please don't say that; haven't I been through enough?" He looked me square in the eyes and declared, "One more miracle, sister, and they will find it in your blood!" I felt compelled to write this epilogue and tell one more story of the miraculous wonder, my ultimate healing and testimony to seal this book. Previously, I had made a decision to leave the details of my affliction out of the story, because I felt that the book's purpose was to glorify God and document the many miracles He had done in my life thus far. My heart was to encourage you to commit your life to serve the living God, and I wanted you to see His greatness. I made the choice not to hinder anyone's faith as they read this book.

Shortly after Brother Love prophesied to me, I began to have symptoms of severe weakness, strange hair loss, and an improperly functioning immune system. As a result, I was getting infections every time there was a change in the weather and suffering from extreme fatigue that caused me to sleep hours at a time just to be able to get up and function. I went to my primary-care physician whom I had seen for years, but he felt that there was nothing wrong with me and that I was reading into things. I changed primary-care physicians and began to see Dr. Wayne Phillip, of Kannapolis Internal Medicine, who cared enough to take my illness seriously. He was the doctor who helped me to get to the root of the problem, referring me to the needed specialists who could identify and treat my declining health. I saw various types of doctors, ranging from dermatologists, rheumatoid specialists and others, who would attempt to diagnose the condition but would only treat symptoms with their unsuccessful attempts; I was in need of a great touch like the woman with the issue of blood: *"a certain woman, which had an issue of blood twelve years, and had suffered many things of many physicians, and had spent all that she had, and was nothing bettered, but rather grew worse"* (Mark 5:25-26). Out of the multitudes around her she pressed in by faith to touch only Jesus. She had to respond to what she heard by faith, and it was her faith that caused her to take action toward God. As the scripture continues, the woman, *"when she had heard of Jesus, came in the press behind, and touched his garment. For she said, If I may touch but his clothes, I shall be whole. And straightway the fountain of her blood was dried up; and she felt in her body that she was healed of that plague. And Jesus, immediately knowing in himself that virtue had gone out of him, turned him about in the press, and said, Who touched my clothes?"* (verses27-30). Her faith moved Jesus so much, *"he looked round about to see her that had done this thing.... And he said unto her, Daughter, thy faith hath made thee whole; go in peace, and be whole of thy plague".* (verses 32, 34). He addressed her as a "daughter," one whom He was deeply acquainted with. She was no longer a "stranger" lost in a crowd, but a "daughter" because of her faith. At that instant, she was made whole, and a brand new life of peace and restoration would follow her all the days of her life. I finally knew what my condition was. After seeing doctor after doctor, the matter was only made worse. I needed the virtue of Jesus to flow within me, for my very life depended on it.

It was the gastroenterologist who first found the tumor on the left side of my abdomen and referred me to a surgeon for a biopsy. The finding of the biopsy was that I had follicular non-hodgkin's lymphoma, which is cancer of the lymph nodes. The doctors who treated me, informed me that this type of lymphoma is a disease that is only treatable, not curable. I was overwhelmed by this diagnosis, but it enlightened me as to the cause of my hair loss and great fatigue. Considering the things I felt God had called me to do, I was reminded of the prophetic word Brother Love spoke over me. Hearing from God gave me the faith to persevere and press in, regardless of the prognosis. I was determined that as long as I had life, I should win as many souls as possible to the Kingdom of God, for if I would take care of God's business, He would take care of mine.

I was now referred to an oncologist to receive more specialized medical attention for lymphoma. The initial treatments were painful, and seemed endless. Recovery from the biopsy took a long time because the incision was very deep. I rolled out of bed every morning with such intense pain that I couldn't even stand up straight and had to use a walker to get around. A new drug called Ritux that is given only to lymphoma patients was recommended, but at best, this treatment could only "possibly" shrink the tumor, offering no assurance. Week in and week out, I would sit with the fluids coursing through my body, and after five treatments, the results of a CAT scan showed little improvement.

The situation looked more disheartening when they recommended a more aggressive treatment. This would include intense chemotherapy and stem cell replacement. It would be a treatment that would be very painful in addition to making me extremely sick, weak and cause me to lose all my hair, if I even survived the process. There were no guarantees; however, it had put some patients into remission. Also, along with chemotherapy, the oncologist told me that I would have to have blood transfusions once a month that would continue after treatment for the rest of my life. As a consolation, he offered me the option of taking the pain medication of my choice, but I refused because of the possibility of being addicted to strong drugs. I wanted my healing to be complete and to glorify God throughout the whole process. He then encouraged me to get a second opinion by speaking to the radiologist.

The radiologist was even more adamant about getting radical treatment quickly since the tumor in my abdomen was the size of a grapefruit and remained a great threat to my life. He believed he could shrink the tumor, but also warned that once radiation is given, the cancer normally shows up in the body somewhere else. That gave me a little hope, but instead of scheduling the treatment, I kept a previous appointment to perform a wedding ceremony at the beach, and spent time seeking God for direction and wisdom.

I recruited all of my friends to pray for me. I was totally against chemotherapy and stem cell replacement as an option for treatment. Knowing that my body could not withstand the medication, there would not be anyone to take care of me while I was undergoing therapy. As a last resort, I searched for information on the prognosis and treatment options available. Much to my dismay, I heard the same information from Duke Medical Center and other specialists.

At that time I decided not to receive treatment, but to continue to pursue the work of the ministry. I resolved to keep preaching, to go to the mission fields, and to complete the writing of this book. Fully persuaded that God had a plan for me, I felt like the four lepers mentioned in the seventh chapter of 2 Kings who stated, "Why sit we here until we die?" Therefore, I continued to fulfill the purpose of God in my life, going on two of the mission trips already written about in this book and writing the book with more passion and determination.

Even so, as the book was progressing, I was beginning to feel much weaker and began experiencing extreme pain. By divine appointment, I had the opportunity to meet another very special oncologist named Dr. Gary Frenette, one of the leading cancer specialists practicing medicine at the Carolina Hematology Clinic located in Charlotte, North Carolina. He suggested that I should have a PET scan, a more detailed state-of-the-art test, which was far superior to what was offered at North East Medical Center at that time. The test results indicated that there were additional tumors; so eight treatments of Ritux were scheduled, with the understanding that it might not work. However, we would give this treatment option one more chance, since it had far fewer side effects than the other treatments mentioned.

During my initial treatments at the Carolina Hematology Clinic in Charlotte, North Carolina, I knew that I had to get people with like faith to be in agreement with me in prayer. Many of my dear friends prayed, fasted and believed for my healing, to whom I will always be very grateful. I also wanted to be in an atmosphere where there was great faith for healings, so I scheduled two trips to see Reverend Ernest Angley in Ohio, who is known to have a great anointing for healing. The first time I went to see him I had a supernatural encounter as I worshiped the Lord with my hands lifted up and tears streaming down my face. Like hot oil being poured from a vessel, I began to experience the sensation of liquid fire pouring from the top of my head to the bottom of my stomach. I knew that the Lord was touching me and witnessed in my spirit that it was a sovereign act of God to release my healing. As I left that meeting, I knew that a miracle was imminent. I started the treatments, and then I went for a second time to see Ernest Angley. This time he laid hands on me and prayed for me. He asked me, "Sister, do you believe that God will heal you?" I said, "Yes, I do believe that God will heal me." Then he replied, "I do too." The next thing I knew, I was lying on the ground under the manifested power of God.

Many other ministers prayed for me, prophetically speaking great faith and promise over me during this time. I continued to go through my scheduled treatments. Sitting in a recliner with IVs of Ritux coursing through me, I would listen for hours to the Word of God on CD through my headset. Instead of focusing on the illness, I would build my faith listening to preachers like Benny Hinn and Paula White.

Interestingly enough, there were others suggesting alternative remedies. I felt it was necessary to briefly address this matter, because we live in a time when there are many voices out there, but we must be very careful not to open our spirits to everything that is available. We need to inquire of God, and ask the Holy Spirit to guide us, especially in a time of intense vulnerability. These unconventional means can border on New Age philosophies or cultic beliefs manifesting strange phenomena. I refused this counsel, because I know that Jesus Christ is the only one who paid the ultimate price for my healing, and He is the only true author of divine miracles today.

The Word of God, along with the combined faith of the friends and ministries agreeing with me, imparted great faith to me in the midst of my trial. Mark 11: 22-24 states, *"And Jesus answering saith unto them, Have faith in God. For verily I say unto you, That whosoever shall say unto this mountain, Be thou removed, and be thou cast into the sea; and shall not doubt in his heart, but shall believe that those things which he saith shall come to pass; he shall have whatsoever he saith. Therefore I say unto you, What things soever ye desire, when ye pray, believe that ye receive them, and ye shall have them"*. I stood on the Word of God daily, commanding the mountain of cancer to leave my body. As I kept speaking, I believed that I was receiving total healing from the cancerous tumors. Cancer is but a small thing in comparison to our Healer, the one and only true and living God. I spoke believing, not doubting in my heart, and I avoided those who conveyed unbelief.

I know that there is purpose for my life, because my work on earth is not yet completed. First, God commissioned me to write this book and I had yet to finish it. There are many souls out there needing deliverance and salvation. There are also the children, little orphans that need the impartation of a mother's love and the revelation of Jesus Christ. Unfulfilled promises that I made to God and my daughter confirmed to me even more that it is not my time to go. In Philippians 1:23-25, Paul the Apostle declared: *"For I am in a strait betwixt two, having a desire to depart, and to be with Christ; which is far better: nevertheless to abide in the flesh is more needful for you. And having this confidence, I know that I shall abide and continue with you all for your furtherance and joy of faith"* (KJV).

So in faith I continued to press on, and the book is finally completed and forwarded to the publisher. As the book is still in the editing stages, I have received the glorious news! Approximately six months after treatments were completed, I was scheduled to have another PET scan. A few days before the test, John, a friend of mine, called and told me to write this down as a witness and testimony of God's miraculous power. He said, "Trish, you are healed of cancer; you don't have it anymore!" As I prepared for the PET scan, I asked the technician to let me pray before the test began, declaring that there would be no more cancer in my body. Agreeing with the Word of the Lord, I believed and had faith to know that the work was accomplished.

A week later, Jade, Patrice's best friend drove me to the doctor's office to receive my test reports. Dr. Frenette came into the room with a big smile on his face and said, "Mrs. Thomas, I have the results of your test, and it is a ***perfect*** scan." I asked him, "What does that mean?" He firmly replied, "Mrs. Thomas, that means you are in complete remission and there is no evidence of the disease in your body! The lymphoma is gone." Jeremiah 30:17a states, *"For I will restore health unto thee, and I will heal thee of thy wounds, saith the LORD"* .

The words of Prophet H. B. Love reverberate in my spirit; "You are going to have need for another miracle before this book is completed....One more miracle, sister, and they will find it in your blood!" I want to convey the power of these words. While I was writing the book, I was stricken with the death sentence of cancer. What the devil meant for evil, even as I was testifying of the miraculous, was that there was *"one more miracle"* I would need. It was not until after the book was completed that my healing was manifested. God gave me the courage and strength to persevere, for we overcome by the blood of the Lamb and the word of our testimony. So the glorious news is that we had to hold the press to proclaim this message! I do not know the specific time this miracle came, because my tests in November still indicated that there were tumors present. I can only speculate that *"the book"* had to be written in black and white. I had to experience again the rejection and pain of unfulfilled dreams; I had to remember the great adversities as well as great victories of His miraculous provision; I had to walk through the heart felt story of my beautiful daughter and our great love for God and for each other; I had to proclaim the story of the hurting children and the cry of the nations who are in desperate need of true love and nurturing; and I had to tell of His rescuing love that will catch your falling soul no matter where you have been or who you are: This is what the good news of the Gospel is all about and this is why He came to earth and died on the cross. For God so loved that He gave....Will you receive? It is free to anyone who will believe— just open your heart.

Jesus said in John 11:4, *"This sickness is not unto death, but for the glory of God, that the Son of God might be glorified thereby"*. Only Jesus Christ, the Great Physician of all physicians, our miracle-working Savior and Lord and only true God, has the power to perform *Miracles, Miracles and More Miracles*.